Our Uncle Sam:

The Sam Cooke Story
From His Family's Perspective

by

Erik Greene

Order this book online at www.trafford.com
or email orders@trafford.com

Most Trafford titles are also available at major online book retailers.

Print information available on the last page.

ISBN: 978-1-4120-6498-9 (sc)
ISBN: 978-1-4122-0987-8 (e)

Picture Credits
Cover: Sam at home in Los Angeles, 1964. Notice how the pattern of the couch matches that of the wallpaper.
(Photograph ©1978 Wallace Seawell/MPTV.net)

Back Cover: Portrait of Sam, untitled, by Maya Escobar.

Trafford rev. 09/14/2020

www.trafford.com
North America & international
toll-free: 844-688-6899 (USA & Canada)
fax: 812 355 4082

To "G", for being there no matter what…

To my Grandfather, Mack E. Greene, my
favorite person in this whole wide world.

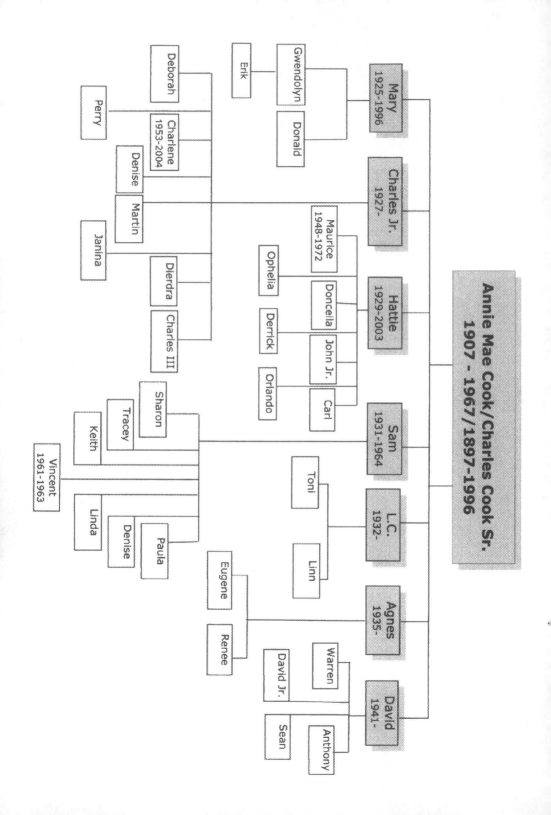

Annie Mae Cook/Charles Cook Sr.
1907 - 1967/1897-1996

Mary
1925-1996

Gwendolyn
Erik

Donald

Deborah

Charlene
1953-2004
Denise

Perry

Martin

Janina

Charles Jr.
1927-

Maurice
1948-1972

Ophelia

Doncella

Derrick

John Jr.

Orlando

Carl

Dierdra

Charles III

Hattie
1929-2003

Sam
1931-1964

Sharon

Tracey

Keith

Vincent
1961-1963

Linda

Denise

Paula

L.C.
1932-

Toni

Linn

Agnes
1935-

Eugene

Renee

Warren

David Jr.

Anthony

Sean

David
1941-

Forward

THIS BOOK IS NOT INTENDED to be the complete Sam Cooke biography. Various authors have combined years of painstaking research and collection of colleague opinion in that pursuit, and while I respect and appreciate their efforts, I do not wish to reiterate them. In contrast, this book will highlight the way Sam's presence, both physically and spiritually, affected and continues to affect my family's lives. I chose to focus on firsthand feelings and memories my family shared about Sam and for that reason tried to include as little outside opinion as possible. The purpose here is to offer Sam Cooke fans around the world a unique perspective to the legendary singer's life, music and death—Sam Cook the man, in addition to Sam Cooke, the artist. My intention is to interject family thoughts and memories about Sam where applicable as I highlight portions of his life and career accomplishments.

Perhaps I should start with a little background on who I am. My mother, Gwendolyn Greene, is the daughter of Sam's oldest sister Mary. As his great nephew, Sam died a year and a half before I was born, hence I never could say I actually knew him. From a literary standpoint, I feel this fact is relevant, but to me it's always been of minor consequence. You see, as with most of my relatives, Sam's spirit lives *within*, and it's carried on by us in our daily lives. My great Aunt Agnes has said "there's not a day that goes by I don't think of Sam," and at the time of this writing it's been forty years since his death. Anyone who has ever felt the impact of his music or the tragedy of his loss understands that sentiment.

My earliest memories of Sam were as a toddler dancing to his music as my mother cleaned our apartment on Chicago's South Side, part of her Saturday morning routine. I'd follow her from room to room (as would Sam's music), picking up lyrics and melodies, my mother picking up toys and socks. As a little boy of maybe 4 or 5, I would request certain favorites:

"Play THAT one again, ma!"

She'd smile, feeling the warmth of my appreciation, and oblige my wish. Later in life she'd admit how amazing it was I could have the same passion for Sam's music as she had, but at such an early age. I, in turn, admitted his music had a captivating essence, whether slow or up-tempo, Gospel or Pop. We surmised it was because many of Sam's songs, especially the ones he wrote, had an enduring quality that seemed to relate to the old and young alike.

By 10 or 11, I knew all the words to his major hits and would sing along, but during this period I began to notice my mother's reaction to Sam's music more intently. Sweeping to "I Belong to Your Heart," for instance, was almost impossible. The broomstick would become a night club microphone, our kitchen floor her stage, and the fluorescent light overhead her spotlight. Vacuuming to "Twistin' the Night Away" would transform our old Hoover upright into an imaginary dance partner a la Fred Astaire and the famous coat rack scene from "Royal Wedding." By this time, stories and memories would accompany some of the songs, and I began to learn of my famous uncle's impact on the music world.

By the time I turned 16, I didn't stick around for mom's "Saturday Morning Revue" too often. My friends and I had discovered that not only were the malls full of 16 year old girls, but that this adolescent nirvana was only 10 minutes away. Plus I found that if I stuck around the house on Saturday morning long enough, she'd inevitably find some sort of chores for me to do. The choice, in my mind, was a simple one. The "Revue," however, continued on without me.

I never gave much thought to Sam's music during my late teens and early 20's. Don't get me wrong, it was always there, constantly being played in the house, but it seemed kind of corny to be a fan of old love ballads and gospel songs when R & B, rap and techno music were what filled black radio airwaves and teenage conversations. In mid-80's Chicago, private parties were dominated by the groundswell of "house music," basically a resurgence of disco songs from the seventies and early eighties. We'd party 'till the wee hours of the morning in underground clubs like the

Playground, the Music Box, or the Power Plant to the mixes of DJ's like Ron Hardy, Frankie Knuckles, or Farley "Funkin'" Keith. It became the norm for amateur DJ's to raid their parent's record collection looking for 10 year old disco songs, scrambling to see who could uncover a hidden "gem" by the next house party. Still I felt embarrassed that "A Change is Gonna Come" could move me to tears or I could play "Bring It On Home to Me" and feel Lou Rawls' background vocals raise the hairs on the nape of my neck. These were feelings I would definitely have to suppress if I were to remain part of the "in" crowd. So I did.

But by my mid 20's Sam's music was back, this time to my rescue. Richard Pryor joked in his standup act that a man doesn't become a MAN until he has had his heart broken; really twisted, chewed up and spit out, he would describe it. In 1991, I became a MAN.

I made the mistake of falling for my ex-girlfriend's best friend, and while girlfriend #1 was no longer in the picture, the guilt and feelings of betrayal girlfriend #2 experienced were too strong and too overwhelming for her to ignore. For over a year, two people who felt they had everything in common yet an insurmountable wall between them played emotional tug-of-war until she one day announced she couldn't take it anymore and had found a new boyfriend to occupy her love interest. A total zombie, I remember returning home from our breakup, walking into our living room and hearing, really *hearing* "Trouble Blues" from the 1963 album "Night Beat." From Sam's humming intro to his very last note, I remember being astonished at how the pain he portrayed in the song seemed to reflect what I was feeling at the time. Over the next two months Sam's music would provide an emotional solace as I learned to appreciate not only the power of his voice but the beauty of his songs as well. "I'll Come Running Back to You," "That's Where It's At," "Only Sixteen," and "Nothin' Can Change This Love" seemed to be written from Sam's pen to my shattered young heart.

Never again would I take his music for granted because it was during that fall of 1991 I realized that sometimes we have to be "blessed" with tragedy in order to develop as human beings. I now understand why my mom wept in a great sense of disbelief in December 1964 when the news broke of Sam's untimely murder, and how these same tears of pain could be turned into tears of pride as she watched her 4 year old son belt out his songs two generations later. During my emotional healing, I played Sam Cooke songs for my closest friends (and potential new girlfriends) and was quite surprised at the warm reaction his music generated. Mind you, it was always a subtle yet well-timed introduction—maybe driving down Lake Shore Drive on a lazy Sunday afternoon or coming home late night from a party—when I'd pull out an unlabelled cassette and pop it into the tape player.

"Here, take a listen to this," I'd say.

The reaction would always be the same—a confused look, a nervous laugh and then silence as they realized this wasn't a joke but that I was sharing a special part of me with them. Some sang along, others tuned it out after a few seconds and continued with conversation, but most listened intently to the melodious voice, the clear diction, and the trademark *whoa-oh-ohs* and smiled, sometimes feeling too embarrassed to ask who the artist was. "It's someone I *should* know," one girl told me. Never once, however, was I asked to turn it off or to see what was playing on the radio. My epiphany was what my mother had seen in my young face several years' prior—good music is eternal and has the ability to transcend all age barriers.

Most recently, I spend my time enjoying the beauty of Sam's "first" career, his days with the Soul Stirrers. It's a testament to his talent how he stepped into the role of lead singer in the famous gospel group at the tender age of 19 and immediately recorded their best-selling record to date, "Peace in the Valley/Jesus Gave Me Water." The Soul Stirrers, Rock & Roll Hall of Fame inductees in their own right, were at the pinnacle of their popularity when Sam was chosen to share the lead with the legendary Paul Foster. In my estimation, some of the finest examples of the human recorded singing voice lie within these 1951-1957 recordings.

So why write this book now? Why after 40 years of silence am I stepping forward to share my family's personal feelings and experiences with

the rest of the world? What compelled me, after decades of family gather-
ings, reunions, and holiday dinners, to remember, record and organize all
the stories passed down over the years? As harsh as it may sound, I didn't
think anyone cared about the Cook family saga but the Cook family. One
event changed all of that.

In 2002, my cousin Marty Cook was surfing the internet and ran
across a Yahoo! Fan Club organizing a tribute. Marty e-mailed my great
aunt, Sam's sister Agnes Hoskins, who in turn, e-mailed the rest of the
family to see if any us of were interested in going to the tribute. When she
received a positive response, she e-mailed Sam Cooke Tribute Foundation
organizer and founding member Reginald McDaniel, identified herself as
Sam's sister, and asked him if they'd mind if a dozen or so family members attended the event. Reggie responded by saying the group would be
honored by our presence and in November of 2002 we were headed to
Atlanta for the "Premier Tribute to Mr. Sam Cooke." David Cook, Sam's
youngest brother, summed up my reaction to that weekend with the three
words he used to open the roundtable discussion: "I am overwhelmed."

In many ways, that weekend opened my eyes to the way fans around
the world saw Sam; they loved him as much as the family members did!
Hence, my family and I owe a great deal of gratitude to the founding
members, organizers and attendees of that event. In addition to Reginald
McDaniel, I'd like to thank Greg Alldredge ("we were going to get together and have a good time, whether there were just three of us or three
hundred of us!"), "Kaptain" Jack Kaplan, Sibyl Kelly and Tami Neat for
not only making it a weekend to remember, but for keeping my uncle's
legacy alive, even more than 50 years after his first recording.

It would be a disservice to exclude fellow "Cookies" Walter Martin,
Lawrence Calvin, Jane Ford, Angela Taylor, Vel Omarr, and Roger Starks
who I met at this first tribute. These are people who, like me, enjoy Sam's
music as part of their daily routine. Special mention goes out to a few
people who made a determined effort to attend, though circumstances
could've very well kept them at home. Kevin Trumper is a gentleman from
Southampton, UK who made the 4,300-mile trip by himself in his first

visit to the United States ever. Jerry Dantzler, who had never flown, heard that a group of people were getting together to honor Sam and bought his first airplane ticket so he wouldn't miss the occasion. Then there's Meni Karoula who's Greek by birth but lives in Canada. Meni describes herself as "Sam Cooke's biggest fan of all time," and based on her passion for Sam's music, I doubt anyone could convincingly win an argument to the contrary! During this brief but spiritually-uplifting weekend my family not only met fans of Sam's music, but established life-long friendships that extend worldwide.

The "Second Annual Sam Cooke Tribute" in September 2003 gave me the pleasure of meeting Clark Kauffman (the founder of the Ultimate Sam Cooke Website), Ireland's Vincent Maloney, Frances Waller, Calvin Graham, and Emily and Amanda Spurlin. Amanda is a college student who was one of the original Fan Club members as a 15 year old high school freshman. I took time to mention all of these Club members because they gave me the impetus to write this book, and I'll thank them eternally for the realization that this effort was indeed necessary.

If you're already a Sam Cooke fan, you have your reasons why and though they may be personal, I highly doubt they're unique. It may have started out with a favorite song, or the fact that you were drawn to the melodious sound of his voice in general. Maybe, like me, he caught you at an intensely emotional period in your life and you found yourself touched by a song or lyric that mirrored your situation completely. Or, you may be new to the Sam Cooke experience and curious to learn about a singer who lived more than half a century ago, but is still shaping popular music today. Regardless, sit back and enjoy a perspective of him that, until now, had been unavailable to the general public. Sam Cooke was more than just a Soul music icon; he was our brother, our cousin, our father, our Uncle Sam.

Chapter One

A Truly Magical Man

"STUDY LONG, STUDY WRONG," SAM barked, squinting from the smoke as he managed to talk around the cigarette dangling from his lips. He leaned back and stretched his arms across the dressing room couch, smiling in admiration as the boy across the table, his 11 yr. old nephew, Maurice, contemplated his next move. Sam calmly tapped the growing ash of his cigarette into a tin ashtray at the end of the couch, but his expression changed to one of concern as the young boy reached for a red checker.

"We *are* playing regular checkers, right?" Sam asked.

The fingers on Maurice's hand recoiled into a fist as he held it over the checkerboard. "Of course we are. What other kind of checkers can you play?"

"That move you were about to make reminded me of Chump Checkers, that's all. But go ahead, since you're sure we're playing regular checkers…" Sam's voice trailed off as he examined his shoe's shine in indifference.

Maurice quickly withdrew his hand. He squinted at Sam, his freckled face trying to guess his uncle's angle. "There ain't no such thing as Chump Checkers!"

Sam looked up as if startled. "Sure it is! It's just the opposite of regular checkers. You try to be the first one to sacrifice all your checkers to the other cat." He paused to wipe an errant ash off of the couch. "Is it my move yet?" he asked, the indifference returning. Sam knew if Maurice really concentrated, he would give him a good game, but that the boy could be easily rattled.

"Don't let him psych you out, Reece!" Sam's nephew Eugene, age 9, chimed in from over his cousin's shoulder, "Go on and make your move! Play *your* game!" Maurice relaxed and went to complete his move with the same red checker.

"Did I ever tell you I met the Chump Checkers Champion?" Sam quickly shot out.

"Chump Checkers Champion?" Maurice asked, his hand frozen in mid air.

Sam now steadied himself for his unrehearsed reply. "He's Chinese, but I met him in Charleston. Ask your Uncle Charles." Sam had to look away briefly, but managed to keep a straight face. "Signed an autograph for him and everything. Big fan."

"Chinese?" Gene asked. With as many people as his uncle knew, anything was possible.

"Absolutely!" Sam beamed. He knew he had them right where he wanted them. "They hold this worldwide tournament every year. The winner gets a gold crown, like a king, 'cause it's still checkers and all, except this crown's worth a million dollars." He leaned in and whispered, as if he had a secret. "Hey! Tell you what. How about I pull some strings and see if I can get y'all into this year's tournament?"

"Man, I don't want to play no Chump Checkers!" Maurice said, hastily moving a different red checker on the opposite side of the board. Sam let out a bellowing laugh, showing the white teeth and smile that had weakened many a young girl's knees over the years.

"You're up, Mr. Cooke." A graveled voice filled the room as an elderly black man poked his head in the dressing room door. The year was 1959 and the noise of the restless crowd in Chicago's Regal Theatre made it seem as if they'd all rushed into the room at that brief instant. Unfazed, Sam leaned forward and intently stared at the wooden pieces, scanning the board one last time until he'd found what he was looking for. Satisfied, his expression relaxed and the million-dollar smile returned.

"Gotta go to work, fellas," he said as he clapped his hands and left the room.

"Gentlemen?" The same graveled voice resonated in the doorway, waiting to escort the boys to their front row seats. They heard the roar of the crowd as their famous uncle was being introduced. Gene broke for the door, not wanting to miss a second of the show, but Maurice's voice stopped him in his tracks.

"Hold up, man," Maurice said, "I wanna make sure we do this right." Maurice's desire to beat his Uncle Sam at checkers was intense. He surveyed the board's configuration, contemplating Sam's countermove, but couldn't concentrate with the old man staring at him.

"Looks good to me," Gene said, nervously tapping his foot and craning his neck towards their impatient escort. "Alright, alright," Maurice said laughing as they both darted for the dressing room door.

An hour and a half and two encores later they would be sitting across the table from Uncle Sam once again. Sam toweled off his sweat-glistened forehead, his silk shirt clinging to his thin frame and chest heaving as he managed to catch his breath. Thousands of frenzied fans were less than 100 ft. away, yet his one focus was finishing the checker game with his young nephew. Sam had spotted the fatal mistake before the show started and smiled as he tripled-jumped Maurice's red checkers, extending the boy's winless streak in one effortless motion. Stunned, Maurice sat frozen for several seconds. By the time he regained his senses, Uncle Sam had been surrounded by friends and family who were laughing loudly and planning the rest of the evening's activities. Maurice sighed, knowing the routine all too well. As the game's loser he folded up the checkerboard and returned the wooden pieces to their coffee can home. To him, it seemed as if Sam's thoughts were now thousands of miles away from their game.

Maurice mindlessly tossed the checkers into the rusted Folgers can, observing the way the growing crowd of people doted on Sam. He realized for the first time that they, too, were consumed by the aura his uncle possessed. To Maurice, Sam was The Man, the epitome of cool. He drove the fanciest cars, wore the slickest clothes and always attracted the prettiest women. The outside world loved his uncle because he was a star, but tonight he noticed Sam seemed truly adored by the people who knew him best. Still, as Sam put on his coat, Maurice could only think about how he'd managed to let yet another checker game slip away. He shot a confused look at Gene. "A million-dollar gold crown for the king of checkers?" The words, spoken aloud, made both boys groan in embarrassment.

"Who are the champion chumps, now?" Sam leaned in and whispered right before being whisked out the door by his entourage. Maurice and Gene laughed, their admiration stronger than ever. Even in defeat they had to admit Uncle Sam was truly a magical man.

And indeed he was. Born to Rev. Charles and Annie Mae Cook (nee Carroll) in Clarksdale, MS on January 22, 1931, Sam Cook was special even as a young child. Famous in the family is the story of how Sam always knew he wanted to become a singer. Sam would plant rows of wooden Popsicle sticks into the ground and sing to them. These sticks would represent his audience. When his 7-year-old brother L.C. asked Sam what he was doing, his answer was that since the average man lived from paycheck to paycheck, it didn't make sense to have a regular 9-to-5 job. Sam's plan was to become a singer. By learning to perform in front of this "audience" he could sing every day, always have money in his pocket, and avoid the financial pitfalls of the common man. Sam, at the time, was all of 9 years old.

Quite often, the phrase "dynamic individual" is used to describe extra-ordinary people. The American Heritage Dictionary defines dynamic as "characterized by progress or activity… by vigor and energy," and the word typically sums up what we want to say about a person who gives above and beyond what is expected of them. To say Sam Cooke was a dynamic individual, however, would be like describing the Universe using the nine planets that make up our solar system; it's a good start, but the expanse left undefined is simply too vast to ignore.

Sam Cooke was one of the most multi-talented, multi-faceted individuals to have lived in the 20th century. It's a bold statement, I'm aware, and one easy to dismiss as biased given the fact that I'm a blood relative. Conversely, it is because of my relation to Sam I can say this. I've compared public information on Sam Cooke to facts and information shared within my family, sifted out the fallacies, and analyzed the remainder in order to get a true sense of where Sam Cooke belongs in my family and in music history. In other words, I make this statement because I've had a chance to examine his legacy, both as a person and as an entertainer, from an "inside" perspective and I'm nothing less than blown away by the lasting effect he's had on so many people's lives. Sam Cooke burst onto the music scene shining as brightly as any star in the darkest sky, and maintained that intensity until his untimely end. It's no wonder that this long after his death, he still has a sizable following worldwide.

To start, Sam Cooke was arguably one of the most prolific entertainers of all time. His voice had a unique resonant clarity that, when he'd hit certain notes, would ring throughout your entire body. Where another singer's voice would be on the verge of cracking, Sam's was as clear as a bell. Because of this unique clarity, Sam's sound hasn't been duplicated since his death, nor may it be anytime soon.

His style developed from a combination of early life experiences and his own personal flavor. Sam honed his gospel skills by singing in church as a child and professionally as a young teenager. This experience, combined with his God-given talent, was why he was able to co-lead the most popular gospel group in his day at only 19 years old. After reaching the pinnacle in spiritual music, he then parlayed his Gospel background into a Pop career. The resulting sound was a unique combination of the two, which is why Sam Cooke is often credited as being the man who invented Soul music.

Sam was also recognized as an accomplished songwriter and producer. As if it weren't impressive enough to have 34 Top 40 R&B hits in his eight years as a Pop star, the fact that he was credited as songwriter on 25 of them is a testament to the talent he possessed in this area. In addition, he penned such Gospel classics as "Touch the Hem of His Garment," "Be with Me Jesus," "Just Another Day," and "That's Heaven to Me" as a member of the Soul Stirrers.

To those fortunate enough to have known Sam Cooke, his persona is what people tend to remember the most, and their descriptions of his traits seemed to run concurrent. He was often described as having a captivating presence, the kind of person whose intense magnetism lit up a room wherever he went. Sam's personality radiated with confidence, and he was charismatic to the point he was often described as "smooth." He could meet you once and address you by your name years later, whether you were a CEO or a guy down on his luck. Sam was an avid reader, an accomplished sketch artist, and a strikingly handsome man that was just as comfortable on a street corner as he was in a business negotiation. Sam had enormous popularity both on stage and off. He was the type of man men wanted to be like and women wanted to be with.

"Sam was the fourth of seven children. He was always outgoing, even as a kid," remembers Agnes, Sam's sister and the matriarch of our family. "Once you met him, you were not a stranger because he became your friend immediately. He was just a bubbly person and anybody he met was a friend until they proved otherwise. He would always have a joke to tell you, no matter what."

"What made his jokes so funny is that he would laugh at them harder than you would!" recalls his youngest brother, David.

"Everyone who met Sam loved him immediately," Agnes adds.

"Even the men loved Sam," his oldest brother Charles remembers. As his personal driver, Charles spent more time on the road with Sam than any other family member. "The fellas would be all over Sam themselves. They just liked him. It wasn't "love" or nothing like that, it was just they liked Sam because he was a cool cat… Women *and* men loved Sam. Sometimes at a show a cat would get mad because his woman was swooning all over Sam and they'd make their way backstage, ready to fight. A few minutes later, they'd be sitting down next to Sam having a drink, saying 'this dude here is al-right!' To this day I've never seen nothing like it."

Sam Cooke went from rags to riches but he wasn't the type of star whose fame, wealth, and notoriety was accompanied by chronic amnesia. He had a heart as big as a whale and his tremendous generosity was another trait by which he's remembered. Sam bought countless cars, furs and jewelry for friends and family members once he made it big. He didn't have to buy his popularity, so the generosity was genuine. Sam made unsolicited donations to black colleges. He traveled with the best musicians in the business, and paid them handsomely. He took care of school tuition expenses for friends and family. He spared no expense to make himself and his surroundings comfortable, and those around him usually reaped the benefits as well. The man had class.

Sam's generosity wasn't limited to just material items. He had a strong sense of family value and made it a point to periodically return to Chicago even though his full time residence was in Los Angeles. Since he was on the road several months a year, both as a Soul Stirrer and as an independent artist, time spent with his family was sacred, especially around the holidays. Because his stays were usually brief, some of the fondest family memories occurred during these special times.

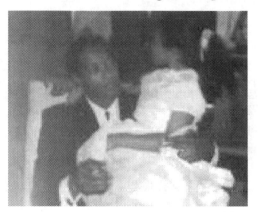

Toni sits with her Uncle Sam, Chicago, 1959.

(Photo courtesy of Toni Cook Howard)

Last but certainly not least, Sam will always be recognized as a pioneer who changed music history, and his legacy is remembered by several monumental "firsts." He is remembered as the first black artist to refuse to sing to segregated audiences. He was the first black recording artist to start his own record label. He was even the first black artist to show cultural pride by shunning the processed look in favor of his natural hair.

Singing as a professional since 16, and being under the tutelage of the middle-aged Soul Stirrers since 19, Sam learned the music business from the inside at a very early age. He understood the power of ownership, whether it was with respect to publishing rights, record labels or management companies, and positioned himself to eventually own and control all three. He took artistic control of his music at a point in time when very few white singers were doing it and certainly no black singers were doing it to his magnitude. Sam Cooke empowered today's artists, both black and white, to avoid the record company rape that was commonplace in the 50's and 60's. Even more impressive, he did all of this before his 34th birthday.

Talented singer, producer, songwriter and arranger; humanitarian, sex symbol and groundbreaking entrepreneur, Sam Cooke was all these things. When the Rock & Roll Hall of Fame opened in 1986, Sam was among the original ten inductees. To get an idea of the magnitude of this honor, The Beatles (1988) and Rolling Stones' (1989) contributions were both recognized *after* Sam Cooke's. In 1987, Sam was inducted into the Songwriters Hall of Fame. In 1993, he was the first recipient of the Pioneer Award from the Rhythm and Blues Foundation. He was awarded a Lifetime Achievement Grammy in 1999, the first of two such posthumous awards. To call Sam Cooke one of the greatest talents of the 20th century may have struck a nerve in some people; especially those who have let the "facts" of his controversial death scar his legacy. But to the people who knew Sam Cook long before he added the show biz "e", it's a compliment that is not only well-earned and well-deserved, but long overdue.

Chapter Two

Like Papa, Like Son

JUST LIKE THOUSANDS OF OTHER sharecrop-era families in the early 1930's, the Reverend Charles Cook, Sr. migrated from Mississippi to the Midwest. In northern cities jobs were plentiful and conditions, though far from ideal, were less harsh than in the oppressive South. The Cooks settled in an apartment on East 36th Street in the Bronzeville neighborhood of Chicago's South Side.

Bronzeville was a 32-square block area overpopulated as a result of black migration and urban segregation. In the thirties, forties and fifties black families were forced to either accept slum-like living conditions in areas like Bronzeville or run the risk of starting a riot by moving into a white community. These blue-collar, segregated neighborhoods often burst at the seams as more and more migrants moved into finite areas, leaving behind a cycle of social and economic plight.

Despite such difficult living conditions, Bronzeville is considered an important part of Chicago's rich cultural history, producing such musical talents as Dinah Washington, Nat "King" Cole and Lou Rawls. Black businesses thrived in a "city within a city" capacity. The publisher of Ebony and Jet magazines John H. Johnson grew up in Bronzeville, as did Alonzo Parham, the first African-American to attend Westpoint. Jazz clubs like the Lincoln Gardens on East 31st Street headlined such names as Joe Oliver and Louis Armstrong in the early 1920's, and by the mid-50's Bronzeville had hosted the likes of Duke Ellington, Count Basie, Miles Davis, Charlie Parker and John Coltrane.

The Cook family was poor but always found a way to make ends meet. "Things were good when we were growing up," Charles, Jr. remembers, speaking as the son of a traveling preacher. "We didn't want for nothing because my daddy always kept a church." As the Pastor's children, the younger Cooks were often doted upon by the church members, especially at Christmastime. "My daddy used to make us give things back at the Christmas parties because the church would be giving us everything. He would tell us 'No. You've got enough.'"

David and Charles remember their fourth-floor apartment as the neighborhood gathering place. "There was always something happening at our house," David reflects. "We didn't have TV back then, so we just entertained at the house." Quite often the apartment would be full of not just Cooks, but with the neighborhood children as well. "If you were hungry, Mama didn't care, she'd just fix you a plate," Charles remembers. "Everybody ate; the whole neighborhood. The house would be full of people every night, and some of them would spend the night. (Mama would say) 'It's late. Go on back there and get in the bed with them boys! Call your mama and tell her you're over here.'"

Agnes remembers that one reason why their home was always full was because Rev. Cook routinely opened his doors to less fortunate children. "When a teenager's parents put them out, they would come to our house." When she ventured to ask her father why, she received a sobering answer. "I asked my daddy 'why do you take in everybody that comes along? There's barely enough room for us!' He said 'your mother and I may be gone one day and you may be on the street. Maybe someone will have to take care of you. That's why I do it.' After that, I never questioned it again."

Rev. Charles Cook, Sr.   *Annie Mae Cook.*
(Photos courtesy of Gwendolyn Greene)

But things weren't always harmonious at the Cook residence. Born 23 months apart, Sam and younger brother L.C. used to fight what seemed like every day, from about age 8 or 9 until they were in their early teens:

Agnes: L.C. was always the stocky one; Sam was always slim and trim, and they were about tit for tat. But they would fight like they were strangers.

David: That's right, I remember that. Sometimes L.C. would win, sometimes Sam would win, but they used to fight *every* day. Now to anybody outside (the family), they were brothers, and Sam would always look out for L.C. But man, they used to go at it!

Agnes: Finally Mama got fed up. When they were in their teens, she told them 'I'm sick and tired of you all fighting!' She made both of them take off their shirts and she whipped them together. They ain't fought since. That was the last fight they had…

Rev. Cook was a strict but loving father. Sunday church services were mandatory for the Cook children, and no one dared question the sunup to sundown weekly routine. The children were not allowed to go to movies or dances (which may have explained Sam's lack of rhythm), and popular music, especially Blues, was strictly forbidden in the Cook household. "You had better not tap your feet to no music if it wasn't church music!" Charles laughs. He was strong-willed and very protective of his family, and let no one intimidate or jeopardize their well being. In other words, Rev. Cook, affectionately known as Papa, "didn't take no mess."

On a routine road trip to Mississippi, for example, Mama Cook packed fried chicken and sliced cake for the trip but hadn't had any bread leaving Chicago. When the family stopped at a gas station along the way, Charles, Mary, and Agnes went into a nearby convenience store to buy a loaf of bread. Charles went to pay for the bread and the man behind the counter asked him "where do you come from boy? Don't you know you don't touch this bread around here, you ask for it." Agnes observed "they didn't touch nothing except the bread they were going to buy. I mean, the bread was already wrapped. It was just a loaf of bread." But when Papa caught wind of the way the store clerk talked to his children, he stormed into the store but didn't have to say a word. "The look on Papa's face said it all," Agnes recalled. "Honey, from the time Papa walked in, that man kept saying 'I'm sorry, I'm sorry! Please, take the bread!' He didn't even charge him for it."

Papa was thin and stood a little less than six feet, but had the presence of a much larger man. "Papa had such a command over his voice, people didn't know what he was going to do," recalls my mother, Gwen. "But by the way he carried himself, he didn't even have to raise his voice for you to know he meant business."

David remembers a trip down South when he was about 7 or 8 years old. Papa had stopped for gas and David went inside the station to buy some candy. "I went in the front door, not knowing about back-door stuff (Jim Crow laws of segregation). When I got halfway through the door, this big redneck started screaming to me at the top of his lungs 'Boy! Just what the hell…'" The poor station clerk never realized Papa Cook was two steps behind his son. "Wait just one minute, now," Papa yelled. "He don't know nothin' about down here!" (referring to unwritten rules of the South). Papa turned and told the attendant "Stop pumping the gas! Stop pumping that gas right now!" and the attendant immediately shut off the pump. He turned back to the clerk and said with fire in his eyes "Don't you ever raise your voice to a child of mine like that again!"

As fiery as Papa Cook was, his wife Annie was the exact opposite in nature. Wed when she was only 16, Mama Cook was a quiet and unassuming woman who had the reputation of living up to her name. She was already famous in the neighborhood for her exploits in the kitchen, and Sam would often brag about his mother's cooking on the road as well. "Everybody would be at our house," David says. "When the Blind Boys came (to Chicago) they would always come to our house." Agnes agreed with this recollection. "My mother would bake rolls that would melt in your mouth. All the singers wanted to come to our house because Sam would be on the road talking about his mother's rolls. When they came to Chicago, they *had* to see the Cook family!"

My mother, an excellent cook in her own right, learned most of her skills from her grandmother. Even as an adult, she's still amazed at her grandmother's culinary wizardry:

"All her meals would consist of a meat, a vegetable, bread, and a dessert. You definitely had a dessert. I remember one time she didn't have a dessert prepared for us ahead of time and Gene kept asking 'what are we gonna have, Grandma?'"

"She could improvise quicker than anyone under the sun. She took white bread, sliced the crust from around it, then pulled down one of her jars of peaches, 'cause she always canned and made jellies, then she added butter and all the seasonings. She put it in the oven, and brother, when that came out... (she closes her eyes, smiles, and shakes her head in the memory) everybody would be smacking their lips! She told Gene 'you know Mama wouldn't let you go without dessert!' Boy, we thought we were in Heaven!"

"She wouldn't have a recipe. It was all by touch. Even when I first got married, I'd say 'OK, Mama, tell me how to prepare this and that.' She'd say 'you just put a little of this in there, a pinch of that...' She never used recipes. It was all creative art..."

Though he was influenced by both parents early in life, Sam picked up his most dominant traits from his father. His movements on stage as well as the way he would wring every emotion out of a song in concert were patterned after the way Papa preached in the pulpit. "When Sam was singing, he used the same mannerisms my dad did when he was preaching," Agnes said, with son Gene nodding in agreement. "If you noticed, he had this hand movement… (she held up one hand and quickly turned her palm back and forth)…that's what Papa did when he was preaching. As a little boy Sam subconsciously patterned himself after my father. What my dad did when he was preaching, Sam did when he sang."

Sam and family. Left to right, Charles, L.C., Papa, Sam, Annie Mae, Hattie, David, Agnes and Gwen.

(*Photo courtesy of Toni Cook Howard*)

Sam shared his father's generosity and tendency to help his fellow man, but the strongest trait he took from Papa Cook was the way he refused to be bullied around by anyone—black or white. Sam was as headstrong as they came and at 5'10" and only 165 lbs., backed down to no one. There was an incident in Memphis, for example, in which a white policeman demanded Sam push his disabled car out of the middle of the road. Sam refused, citing his job as a singer was to push records, not cars. He told the policeman to write a ticket if he had to, he'd pay the fine, but he wasn't pushing the car out of the road. He sat back inside and waited for help, not giving the stunned trooper a second thought.

Sam's boldness shocked me, especially in a time and place where blacks could be beaten by police or lynched by locals for such a rebellious attitude. Naturally it made me ask my aunt and uncle about how true the story could've been. David's nonchalant response was "Sam would do that, now." Agnes, with the same indifference, agreed by saying "I believe it. That sounds like something Sam would do." Still amazed, I asked them "Even in the South?" to which Agnes replied "Even down South! Sam didn't care!"

Sam started singing in Rev. Cook's Christ Temple Church as a boy of eight or nine. The five oldest siblings (Mary, Charles, Hattie, Sam and L.C.) organized a singing group within the church called the Singing Children, with Charles and Mary on lead, Hattie on baritone and L.C. on bass. "(Papa) used to make me sing more than anybody else," Charles remembers. "I'd sing before he'd preach and warm up the church." The group traveled from church to church with Papa and became quite popular. Sam sang tenor, and though he wanted to lead, Mary and Charles refused. "We didn't even take him seriously," Charles would later say.

The novelty of the Singing Children wore off, however, after Sam's freshman year at Wendell Phillips High School. It was during this time he joined a group called the Highway QC's (no one could ever explain why "QC's" or what it stood for, though the name came from the Highway Baptist Church). The group, with Sam's help, made quite a name for themselves singing the local church circuit.

"I went to the Service from '46 to '49 and when I came home they told me Sam was singing with the Highway QC's," Charles recalls. "They were in a church storefront and when I heard Sam I said 'I didn't know that boy could lead like that!' You see, I wouldn't let him lead when he was singing with us. He made a better tenor singer, I thought, than a lead singer. But when I heard him sing lead, boy, I was really shocked!"

Highway QC's, circa 1947: top row—Gus Treadwell, Jake Richard, Marvin Jones. Bottom row—Sam, Creedell Copeland, Lee Richard. (Photo courtesy of Toni Cook Howard)

The first time Charles heard Sam sing and saw the almost hypnotic spell his brother's voice had on a crowd, he knew he was witnessing something truly spectacular. Sam's tenor was sweet and melodious and had that unique "something" that reached inside of you and touched you in places you never knew existed. "His voice contained sincerity," is the way my mother described it. "It sounded innocent, but in a masculine way; strong yet sensitive at the same time. Besides that he was handsome and always pleasant and polite. You should've seen the way Sam made those women in the pews melt like butter! But that was the thing that made him so popular—between his personality and his voice, you were drawn to him. Man or woman, young or old, Sam's voice could make you stop whatever you were doing and give him your undivided attention. He had that effect. He'd have the whole church mesmerized; hanging on every word. He sang with a depth that was so intense, at the end of a song he left you speechless except for one word: 'Yes!'"

"They were a very young group, all teenagers," Agnes states, her eyes lighting up as she relives the Highway QC years. "Whenever they would go to a Soul Stirrers program, they would sit in the audience and the Soul Stirrers would not call them onto the stage. The people in the audience would start yelling 'the QC's are in the house! The QC's are in the house!' Finally, they didn't have a choice but to call them on the stage, and when they got onstage they really turned it out! This is why the Soul Stirrers did not want them to perform on their program. That's also why they recruited Sam to sing with them, because they knew the QC's would tear it up every time. That was really funny, because the Stirrers would act like they didn't even see them, until the audience started yelling! Those were the good times. I was a teenager at the time and everywhere the QC's went, I went. My girlfriend and I followed them religiously."

A teenaged Sam Cook.

(Photo courtesy of Toni Cook Howard)

Sam graduated from Phillips H.S. in the summer of 1948. By this time the QC's were so successful in the city they branched out to churches in other little local towns. The group worked hard on polishing their style and delivery. A year later they would be on the road touring the Midwest and South, with extended stays in Gospel hotbeds such as Detroit and Memphis. As a QC, Sam would practice and rehearse almost to the point where it became an obsession, and he even began to try his hand at songwriting. Sam would write whenever the mood struck, sometimes to the detriment of his youngest brother.

"Sam and I would share a bed when he got off the road," David recalls.

"Sam would get up in the middle of the night and get the Bible. I'm thinking to myself 'Man, I've got to get up and go to school in the morning!'"

Sam's love for music may have only been eclipsed by his love for reading. "In grammar school he would always take the maximum number of books out of the library," Agnes remembered. "Then he would make me go back in and get more books on *my* card!"

On the road, Sam passed the long stretches of idle time by reading, and it was a habit he carried into adulthood. "He'd see a drugstore and tell me to stop and he'd buy *every* magazine on the rack," Charles remembers. "It wouldn't matter what it was! Anything that was published, he'd read it. The man behind the counter used to look at us like we were crazy, but Sam would read every last one of those magazines from cover to cover. He'd retain it all, too. He could hold a conversation about any subject you brought up."

Sam would always credit his songwriting ability to his voracious appetite for books. His wide range of interests spanned from the classics to African history to world politics. "Sam told me to always read and always stay in school," David said. "And after watching his accomplishments, I had no choice but to say 'OK, Sam!'"

Sam's formative years spent touring with the QC's were an early glimpse of how life on the road was for a gospel singer. Quite often, they lived at second-rate motels and depended upon fast food for their meals. If they were lucky, a promoter or church parishioner would invite them to a home-cooked meal. But it was the life his father knew as an itinerant preacher, and he had left with Papa's blessing. After all, Papa himself had fed the Cook family for years with this type of lifestyle before establishing a "secure" home at Christ Temple Church in suburban Chicago Heights.

The year and a half the group spent on the road had not only been grueling, but a lesson in futility as well. With their crisp uniforms and even crisper harmonies, the Highway QC's were still seen as a younger version of the Soul Stirrers, and though they were respected on the gospel front in their own right, the group couldn't seem to shake the Soul Stirrers' shadow. Then a door opened which helped catapult Sam's career.

Chapter Three

The Soul Stirrer Years

IN DECEMBER OF 1950, THE legendary Rebert H. Harris shocked the gospel world by announcing his retirement as lead singer of the Soul Stirrers. This news was disastrous—it would send a ripple effect not only through the group but their new record company, Specialty Records, as well. To replace an immense talent such as R.H. Harris was almost impossible, or so the group thought.

After scrambling around rehearsing replacements, the veteran group reluctantly decided to hire Cook a month before his 20th birthday to complement Paul Foster in their two-lead arrangement. Sam had been a hit on the "juvenile circuit", so much so that the Stirrers intentionally ignored the QC's at their shows in respect of Sam's talent, but the group was still understandably concerned. First of all, the pressure was on them to find a replacement that would not just satisfy, but electrify, as R.H. Harris had done for years. Secondly, they had just signed a new recording contract and the label owner, thinking he had bought the "complete package", had not been immediately informed of Harris' departure. Finally, to bring Sam Cook in would mean the group would have to rely on an untested teenager for their livelihood. Most of the present members had been singing together since Sam was in kindergarten, so this was a move that could make or break the group. Could the boy step in and handle the pressures of "big league" Gospel life?

On the other side of the coin, Sam's decision to accept the Stirrers' invitation wasn't as clear cut as one would imagine. Sam had great reservations about leaving behind a group he had become friends and grown up with. Sam was a year or two older than the rest of the Highway QC's and he realized they looked up to him and would take the news hard.

"When the Soul Stirrers approached him, he asked me 'man, what do you think I should do?'" Charles retells the conversation. "'Do you think I should go with the Soul Stirrers? I hate to leave and break up my group.' I told him 'you gotta look out for yourself. Go with the Soul Stirrers.' Boy, them Highway QC's cried so hard…!"

All doubts and fears subsided by the summer of 1951, when Specialty released the first single from the revamped Soul Stirrers. "Peace in the Valley/Jesus Gave Me Water" was an instant hit and ended up selling more than 65,000 copies. To give you an idea of its impact in the gospel community, sales more than doubled the 27,000 copies their best-selling Harris-lead single, "By and By," sold the year before. The bright-eyed 20-year-old Cook had achieved what at one time seemed impossible; acceptance by the group and the fans as well. "They couldn't keep that record in," Charles recalls. "The record shop was right around the corner from us and the man told me 'I can't keep 'em in.'"

"Jesus Gave Me Water" showed the gospel world a glimpse of the enormous talent Sam Cook possessed. The bold confidence with which he attacked the song was unheard of at the time. He danced around the word "water," ad libbing it to the point he described it as "living, loving, lasting water," repeating it as if he were being baptized by the word itself. The gospel crowd was initially stunned until they realized how refreshingly wonderful Sam made the song sound. R.H. Harris' solemn, traditional version of the song had been no match for Sam Cook's innovative, happy-go-lucky approach.

"People always try and say 'R.H. Harris taught Sam how to sing.'" Charles states, his voice full of contempt. "R.H. Harris ain't taught Sam to sing no more than a man on the moon. Sam developed his *own* style. R.H. Harris was a great one, don't get me wrong, but *nobody* else had a style like Sam's."

Soul Stirrers promotional photo, 1951. From top to bottom, Sam, R. B. Robinson, Paul Foster, S.R. Crain, Jesse "J.J." Farley. (Photo courtesy of Dorothy Holloway Coates) Inset photo, circa 1952, shows clockwise, Crain, Sam, Farley, Foster and Robinson.

(Photo courtesy of Toni Cook Howard)

Listening to the songs Sam recorded with the Soul Stirrers is like having a rich chocolate fudge cake all to yourself—you want to eat it all at once, but you know it's best to enjoy it slowly. And even if you did eat the cake in one sitting, the resulting stomach ache would probably hurt so good, it would all be worth it.

Part of the why the Soul Stirrer's gospel sound was so captivating had as much to do with their pinpoint harmonies as it did their spiritual subject matter. I have always said you don't have to be a fan of the "oldies," or even a fan of gospel music, to appreciate their skill and expertise. They sang tightly as a group yet shined individually.

The key to the Soul Stirrers' appeal could be found in their early a cappella recordings—they maintained a disciplined unison yet each member's contribution could be clearly identified. Paul Foster's battle-tested experience contrasted Sam's youthful energy on songs like "It Wont Be Very Long," helping establish a distinct new sound in Gospel. Jesse "J.J." Farley's deep, rich bass held the tempo with a "boom, boom, boom" repetition on songs like "Jesus Done Just What He Said" and "I'm Gonna Build On that Shore." The sweet harmonization between first tenor S.R. Crain and baritones Thomas Bruster and R.B. Robinson is showcased on songs like "Christ is All," "Joy, Joy to My Soul" and "He's My Rock." In their a cappella songs, the background members not only complemented the lead singers, their voices provided the "music" necessary in establishing the rhythm as well.

Later, when the group added instruments, their harmonizing skills were downplayed as the tempo was now carried by drumbeat. These changes gave the lead singers increased exposure and allowed the group to experiment with more creative vocal arrangements. Sam's intentional false-start delivery was a refreshing twist as he traded leads with Paul Foster on "I Gave Up Everything to Follow Him." He exuded a comfortable confidence in the 1955 classic "The Last Mile of the Way" as he took the word "mile" up through the heavens before letting it fall gently back to earth. And when Sam and Paul traded leads on the 1956 single "Must Jesus Bear This Cross Alone?," Sam initially answered Paul, they switched roles and Sam became the lead, then they switched *back* in an exchange so seamless it was virtually undetectable. It was the little complexities made the Soul Stirrers great, and at their best they were as smooth as any group that ever existed.

Sam as a young Soul Stirrer, 1953.
(Photo courtesy of Joe Cook)

Paul Foster and J.J. Farley
(Photo courtesy of Charlene Graham)

"When Sam would sing at DuSable (H.S.), the neighborhood would be empty," Charles laughs. "The storeowners would say 'your brother must've been singing in town somewhere, because we haven't hardly had no business!' Their business would fall off because everybody would try to get to the program early to get a good seat. Thirty-Sixth Street would be lined up with people before the doors even opened."

I once loaned a CD I had made to a friend who sings in a gospel choir but was unfamiliar with the Soul Stirrers experience. I didn't ask directly, but I wanted him to analyze and grade their performance. The songs were recorded before we both were born, but I knew that if anyone could appreciate their musical value, it would be him. As he scanned the titles, he immediately recognized songs like "Peace in the Valley," "Just Another Day," and "Farther Along," and even admitted his choir still sang "Jesus, I'll Never Forget." I figured I'd give him a week or two to let the songs soak in, then ask him what he thought. Needless to say I was shocked when a half hour later he called me to say he was playing the CD in his car and had to pull over to avoid running off the road. As a veteran participant of a traveling gospel choir, he could appreciate the dedication it took the Soul Stirrers to hone their skills to razor sharpness. He admitted he'd heard groups who'd sung together for years and never came close to their precision. He embarrassedly confessed that he started to call me after listening to the first track, but wanted to hear more. It seems he, too, was tempted to devour that rich chocolate fudge cake in just one sitting!

In bittersweet irony, "Peace in the Valley/Jesus Gave Me Water" represented the pinnacle of the group's success, though the blame wasn't entirely their own. The Great Black Migration reshaped the mainstream musical landscape in the late '40's and early '50's as new styles of music gained popularity. Fueled by failing crops, industrial demand for factory workers, and Southern discrimination, the Migration started around 1915 and attracted blacks to northern cities throughout the 1950's. Chicago, for example, saw its African-American population increase 250% between 1910 and 1920 alone.

Blues and Jazz musicians, who migrated from cities like Memphis and New Orleans, began to make their mark on the Chicago music scene. Gospel music now had formidable competition, as evidenced by the need to replace the term "race" records with the more politically-correct term "Rhythm & Blues," or R&B for short. Louis Jordan, dubbed "The Father of Rhythm & Blues," had 18 number one singles between 1943 and 1950. Fats Domino would rule the 1950's charting 59 R & B singles—37 of them Top 40.

Many of these early "underground" R&B songs had graphic sexual undertones. Titles to songs like Wynonie Harris' 1948 classic "Good Rockin' Tonight," as well as Julia Lee's "King Size Papa" and "My Man Stands Out" left little to the imagination, yet flew beneath the obscenity radar because their popularity remained mainly within the Negro community. But in 1951, The Dominoes recorded the first crossover hit when the controversial "60 Minute Man" spilled onto the Pop charts, topping out at #17. In the song, Domino bass singer Bill Brown bragged "I rock 'em, roll 'em, all night long," thus giving birth to the term "rock & roll." Much like the effect Gangster Rap would have in the late '80's, the proverbial "smut pot" had boiled over into mainstream America.

So where did all of this leave the Soul Stirrers and the direction of Gospel music in general? How could a group of men who stood rather motionless as they sang disciplined harmonies compete with the wild new craze on the horizon? Why should it have to? R&B and Rock and Roll were in their infancy and their impact on Gospel may not have been inherently obvious at first. The effect, however, was dwindling record sales due to the declining number of young listeners. Whereas Gospel was stoic and often focused on death, sin, and the afterlife, Rock and Roll was fresh, liberating, and rebellious. Fortunately, the Soul Stirrers were better off than other gospel acts—their talented, handsome lead singer attracted plenty of young women to their shows—but as polished and established as the Soul Stirrers were, they had to adapt to changing times as well. Danceable rhythms, suggestive lyrics and twisting dance moves were out of the question, so the group (and the music) had to find other ways to evolve.

If one follows the Stirrer sessions chronologically, it is interesting to watch how the group's serious sound became more and more relaxed, more *mainstream*, as the years went by. Out of the 11 songs in Sam's first recording session on March 1, 1951, all but one alternate take of "I'm On the Firing Line" was a cappella. Singing a cappella best showcased the Soul Stirrer's harmonizing skills, and Sam's carefree style lent a youthful exuberance to a group of men old enough to be his father. While the Stirrers sang with religious purpose behind R.H. Harris, Sam dared to attack songs like "Jesus Gave Me Water" in a nonchalant manner that was borderline playful.

Sam's signed picture to his sister Mary.

(Photo courtesy of Gwendolyn Greene)

*National Quartet Convention, Los Angeles, August 1952. Top row: a friend named
Ella, Charles, a friend named Eunice, Sam, and Barbara Bonner.
Bottom row: Lou Rawls and L.C.*

(Photo courtesy of Toni Cook Howard)

Their next recording session came nearly a year later in February of
1952. By then, Sam sang with more confidence as his singing voice started to mature. This session produced a version of "How Far Am I from
Canaan?" that Specialty Owner and A&R Art Rupe felt had commercial
appeal. In the unreleased March 1951 version, Sam sounds still unsure of
his talent by trying to make.sure.he.said.each.word.clearly.and.distinctly.
A year later, he sang the song as if he were ashamed it ever presented a
challenge. Even Rupe had to comment that their performance that day
was worthy of "three A's and a +."

By this time, the group was experimenting with a snare accompaniment as well as different tempos to create a more "modern" sound. For
example, they recorded a slow, somber take of "Let Me Go Home" that
was dark and depressing when compared to the more upbeat final version.
In later sessions Specialty's arrangers would add piano and organ accom-

paniments, and eventually, on songs like "Come and Go to that Land," an electric guitar. Art Rupe knew that even though it was important that sacred music remain sacred (i.e. not be confused with "Pop"), radical but necessary advancements had to be made in order to help sagging record sales. However, try as they might, the Sam Cooke-era Soul Stirrers never had another single as successful as their very first one.

For Sam, life on the Gospel Highway provided him with invaluable experiences that would eventually fuel his commercial success. The average Soul Stirrer fan only saw the "finished product" at a gospel show—an assembly of neatly-uniformed men melodiously singing praises in their Lord Jesus' name. Behind the scenes, however, there was a great deal of preparation that went into making that finished product possible. The group members had to act as their own accountants, booking agents, and treasurers. The men set their own rules and enforced them with monetary fines. They had to budget for food, travel time, hotels, gasoline, car maintenance, *and* the possibility of getting stiffed on a performance. In addition, they were signed to a recording contract, and though road shows were their main source of income, they ultimately were held accountable for whatever royalties they negotiated. Senior Roy Crain was not only the Stirrers' first tenor and songwriter, but their Road Manager as well. Sam intently studied the aspects of running a business from him, and as a result acquired knowledge beyond his years. Sam Cook learned the music business long before he was *supposed* to learn it.

The Gospel Highway taught Sam lessons in responsibility as well. One fact almost impossible to ignore was the increase in young women at gospel programs, both in Chicago and on the road, and how they would readily make themselves available to Sam. Long before pop music made him a household name, even as far back as the Highway QC's, it was a known fact in music circles that Sam Cook could have just about any woman he wanted, and he turned down many more offers than he accepted. "Sam liked the fine, young innocent girls," Charles remembers. Besides his talents on stage, Sam's good looks and charming personality undoubtedly contributed to his sexual attraction. Women routinely threw themselves at Sam, and often he found himself in the enviable position to be able to pick from the cream of every church's crop.

In the fifties, the true test of a gospel singer or gospel group was its ability to make its listeners, particularly the women in the audience, catch the "Holy Ghost." The more passionately you sang, the more likely the Holy Ghost would appear in the audience. By the same token, the more passionately you sang, the more likely the young women would appear at your dressing room door. To those not familiar with church spirit in general or black church spirit in particular, the Holy Ghost is the great rush of emotion one experiences during reception of God's word, whether spoken or in song. Its effect can result in dancing, moaning, screaming, or sobbing, and climaxes as a cathartic ecstasy. An extreme case of Holy Ghost leaves one emotionally and physically spent, not unlike an extreme orgasm. In fact, there is a fine line between the Holy Ghost experience and the orgasmic experience, a line that is often crossed in the church pew itself. To the kind of singer whose hypnotic voice routinely induced these orgasmic convulsions, it's not surprising an entourage of willing young women was always at his beck and call.

This being said, and not to offend the church regulars, there are potholes on most stretches of highway, and the Gospel Highway was no different. In April of 1953, Sam found himself in a rather precarious situation—three women in two cities were having his babies at the same time. In Chicago, Evelyn Jackson welcomed into the world Sam's daughter Paula on April 8th, while childhood sweetheart Barbara Campbell gave birth to his daughter Linda on the 25th. In Cleveland, Marine Somerville was busy giving birth to still a third daughter, Denise, who was born on the 23rd.

Soul Stirrers Souvenir Program, 1955.

(Program courtesy of Toni Cook Howard)

I naturally wondered what Papa's reaction to his son having three children out of wedlock would be. He was a stern believer in the idea that if a girl was in a "family way," a wedding shouldn't be too distant in the future. But surprisingly, Papa didn't hold Sam to the same standards he would have held his other children or grandchildren. Or if he did, no one in the family remembers Papa stressing to Sam to "do the right thing" (Sam would eventually marry Barbara Campbell in 1959). Perhaps it was because there were multiple women involved and there was no clear cut "right thing." Perhaps this was the more "understanding" Papa whose disciplined nature gradually softened as the years went by. Or even still, Papa may have understood the inherent temptations of Sam's lifestyle, having spent years on the road as a traveling preacher himself. Regardless, Sam always made his family aware if there were any additions, and Papa Cook made sure he acknowledged the grandchildren as his own.

"Papa kept up with his grandchildren because he was really concerned about them," Agnes admits. "He'd visit the ones that were in the city, like Paula. Paula's stepfather didn't want her to have anything to do with the family because he was jealous of Sam's fame. Papa said he wasn't thinking about him, because Paula was his grandchild. Papa would go there anyway. Evelyn said that Papa would just come on in and ignore her husband. If he'd speak, Papa would speak, if not, Papa would just visit with Paula and that was it."

In the summer of 1953 the Soul Stirrers found themselves on tour in California, but for Sam, Fresno was memorable for more than just their Memorial Auditorium performance. After the show, a stunningly attractive young singer named Delores Mohawk sought out the closest Stirrer she could find, S.R. Crain in this case, and requested a formal introduction to Sam Cook.

Born Delores Milligan some twenty-three years earlier, her friends and family called her Lois, but Sam preferred to call her Dee-Dee. Even in casual conversation it was obvious Dee-Dee had experienced more in life than most women her age. As a teenager in 1948, she gave birth to a son named Joey, and by the time she met Sam, had married and divorced a man named Nathaniel Brown. She supported herself by singing with a local band, working as a secretary, and waiting tables at a family-owned restaurant/tavern. Somewhere along the line she decided to honor her Indian heritage and changed her last name to Mohawk. Despite her colorful past, Sam took an immediate liking to Dee-Dee, and spent the next several days with her in Fresno before catching up with the Soul Stirrers for their show in Oakland.

In October of 1953 the couple married and virtually overnight Sam had become a full-fledged family man. That fall, with vacancy in Bronzeville scarce, Sam would move Dee-Dee and Joey into his basement apartment on 65th St., but not before making a triumphant return to Fresno to claim his bride. Joe Cook, with help from older relatives, recalls the commotion Sam caused as he made his way through the sleepy, rural town:

"Sam pulled into Fresno in a long Cadillac with three or four other nice cars, all Cadillacs, I believe, trailing behind. The local town people saw this caravan and just joined in, curious to know what was going on. Pretty soon there were 25-30 cars all lined up heading to my aunt's house."

"Word got around quickly in Fresno if someone, especially someone of color, was new in town," Joe continued. The sight of the caravan attracted locals from everywhere, and before long the crowd congregated just outside his Aunt Elizabeth's Valencia Street home. "I remember my mom opening the shades and seeing wall-to-wall eyeballs in the window. People were standing on fences and climbing up trees and telephone poles just to get a look at Sam. There were, I'd say, between 200-300 people surrounding the house. My aunt was concerned they were going to tear the whole place down."

The Cook family successfully managed to escape Fresno and complete their pilgrimage to Chicago's South Side. As an adult Joe Cook had these memories to share about the brief five years he lived with his father:

"I remember my first Thanksgiving in Chicago, over at Mama Cook's house. I didn't know the other kids and they didn't know me. They were all whispering around the table until she made them each line up and give me a hug and welcome me to the family..."

Delores Mohawk Cook.

(Photos courtesy of Joe Cook,
* courtesy of Toni Cook Howard)

Sam's signed picture to Dee-Dee.

(Photos courtesy of Joe Cook)

Sam and Dee-Dee in Fresno, 1953.

(Photos courtesy of Joe Cook)

"Even as a little boy, I remember the incredible magnetism Sam had. Everyone wanted to get a piece of him. People just wanted to touch him, to get next to him. You could never get enough of Sam because so many people wanted him."

"One thing about Sam, he never hesitated to introduce me to celebrities or crowds of people as his son Joey. He always made me feel warm inside, always made me feel like his son. One time, he brought me onstage at the Apollo Theatre after a gospel review. They wanted to introduce the family members of all the groups that performed and I was terrified. They called my name '…we want to introduce little Joey Cook…come on out, Joey!' I looked out at the crowd and said 'I ain't going out there!' Sam looked over at me and gave a little nudge with his head and said 'come on out here, son.' I walked out there, took a little bow, and the crowd started cheering. He put his arms around me and I realized that everything was alright. He could make you do things you wouldn't normally do. Like I've never been comfortable talking in front of crowds, but when I was around him, I could do it. I didn't have any fear whatsoever when he was around. He made me feel just that comfortable and confident. He made me *want* to do things to impress him."

"Maybe he overcompensated because he was on the road so much, I don't know, but I used to push my luck with Sam a lot of times because I knew he would do things for me. One time we went to a sporting goods store and I rode out of there on the most expensive bike they had. He bought me a dog when we were on the road, even though the hotel we were staying in didn't allow dogs. He had to sneak it in under his coat, but he wanted me to have that dog. (Joey would name him Newark since the dog hailed from the New Jersey city). Sam and my mom would dress me like a little prince. I had suede coats, the nicest shoes. I even had a little red smoking jacket before that guy from Playboy did!"

Sam and Dee-Dee would stay married for five years, but over the course of time Sam's extended road tours eventually took their toll. "My mom was really something special," Joe reflects. "She had a lot of pressure with Sam being gone six to eight weeks at a time. He made money with the Soul Stirrers, but sometimes it wasn't enough. Those guys had to chip in and buy matching suits and shoes, or buy a new car to travel in every year or so. Things got better after "You Send Me" hit it big, but before that my mom was a real trooper because she stuck it out. She worked in a bar, she worked as a secretary. She even had a job at a bowling alley at one point. She did whatever it took to make ends meet."

After the marriage dissolved, Dee-Dee and Joey moved back to Fresno where she died in an automobile accident soon afterward. "Mom deserved to get a lot more out of life than she did," Joe laments. He was taken in by an uncle who would change his name to that of Dee-Dee's first husband and he became Nathaniel Brown, Jr. His uncle, like Paula Jackson's step-father in Chicago, discouraged Sam's involvement in Joey's life and the two would have little interaction over the years. But Joe remembers "Sam was always good to me, always treated me like his son. Sam was the only man I ever called Dad."

By the mid-50's, Sam was a seasoned veteran both on the road and in the studio, and had taken on a larger part within the Soul Stirrers as both arranger and songwriter. In an August 1955 session, the Stirrers recorded the upbeat, Cooke-penned, "He's My Guide." Though never released as a single, the song probably came closer to crossing the Pop line than any other song to date. Sam and co-lead Paul Foster traded shouts in a song which is light, airy, and fun, with the focus remaining on Jesus Christ as their mutual savior. This song, along with two songs Sam would write later, "That's Heaven to Me" and "Touch the Hem of His Garment," showed that Gospel music could break away from its traditional sound and still effectively carry the word of God.

Christmas, 1953 in Chicago. R.B. Robinson's son Bernard, Barbara Bonner, Joey Cook.
Barbara would later marry Sam's brother L.C.

(Photo courtesy of Joe Cook)

Joey and his dog, Newark,
 age 7, 1955.
(Photo courtesy of Joe Cook.)

Dee-Dee and Joey.
(Photo courtesy of Gwendolyn Greene)

Specialty released "Nearer To Thee/Be With Me Jesus" from the August 1955 session. With 37,000 singles sold, it was the most successful release since "Peace in the Valley/Jesus Gave Me Water" and it represented the first time the Soul Stirrers released a single with both sides written by Sam Cook. Though Sam shared the lead with Paul on "Be With Me Jesus," he had clearly become the central figure in the group. Still only 24, he had risen to the top of the ranks in Gospel music yet had the presence of mind to realize that there was more to life than being a Soul Stirrer.

Over time, Sam had become increasingly restless with the fact that he was the star of the group but the money wasn't always divided to reflect this. There was an incident which brought this point to a boil:

"Sam used to split his songwriting royalties with the Soul Stirrers," Charles recalls. "They were Sam's checks. They came in the name 'Sam Cook', not the 'Soul Stirrers', but Sam would split the money with them. Then one day he said 'look fellas, I'm getting ready to move, and I'm going to need this check to move with.' Somebody jumped up, I think it was R.B. Robinson, and said 'you can't do that! We've been splitting that money up until this point.' Sam said 'Oh, yeah? Watch me. I'll be damned if I let you tell me what I can or cannot do with *my* money!' And he meant it!"

"R.B. got mad because Sam wouldn't split the one check?" I asked.

"One check!"

One of the reasons for Robinson's ire may have been because he was renting an apartment to Sam and stood to lose money in two ways, through the split and through the loss of a tenant. Another may have been the realization that Sam Cook was becoming bigger than the Soul Stirrers themselves. Subsequent road shows were tension-filled as the incident undoubtedly created dissension between Sam and R.B. It was around this time Sam started to peek over the fence and see that there was a much more lucrative alternative to this life—an alternative called popular music.

Chapter Four

Pop Goes the Preacher's Son: The Discovery of *You Send Me*

To THE OLDER GOD-FEARING, BIBLE-TOTING black Christian of the 1950's, popular music was considered to be the music of sinners. This was the generation that either migrated from or still lived in the South, where Jazz, Blues, and R&B were associated with late-night juke joints, liquor, loose women and lewd behavior. By the same token, for a singer to consciously abandon his gospel roots for Pop music was seen as making a deal with the Devil.

Sam was from a different generation. As a Soul Stirrer, he began to experiment with Pop songs he had written for fun. On the road, Sam would often grab a guitar and test his material on groups of young women after Soul Stirrer shows, mostly to warm reception and constructive criticism. Once he made up his mind he wanted to try the other side, he knew that selling Art Rupe and the other Stirrers on the idea of recording a couple of Pop demos would be no easy task. The bigger hurdle, however, would be to tell the Rev. Charles Cook, Sr. his intentions.

"Sam had a lot of respect for my dad," Agnes said. "Before he made a major decision, he'd always consult my father first."

As a Gospel neophyte, Sam was happy just to have been given the opportunity to be a Soul Stirrer. But as he matured into the featured lead singer, an established songwriter and arranger, and one of the most recognizable figures in Gospel, his just-happy-to-be-in-the-game euphoria had waned. Didn't he owe it to himself to get the most out of his talent? Had he not paid his dues on the Gospel Highway? Why shouldn't he be the one in control of his own destiny? Convinced of his decision, Sam picked up the phone to call his father.

To Sam's relief, the phone call went surprisingly well. There was no shouting, no screaming, no accusations of "turning your back on your religion." He had concluded the call with his father's coveted blessing, but what he didn't know was that deep down inside, Papa Cook was hurt. "You could see it in his face," Agnes recalled. Regardless, Papa did his best to hide any resentment and truly wished Sam well.

"Papa came to gradually accept it," said David. "Papa changed a lot over the years, because, man, growing up, Papa didn't allow us to go to the movies, we couldn't go to parties...and as the youngest, I had it easier than Charles and them." Charles chimed in to say "He had it <u>way</u> easier than we did! As the years went by, Papa did get a little softer. His ways of thinking changed. But when you were living under his roof, you danced to his music!" David added "and it better be some church music, 'cause Papa didn't put up with anything else!"

There was also a matter of how his decision would be accepted in the gospel world. "Some people were upset," Agnes recalls. "At the time Sam's minister was Rev. Rawls. I don't think it bothered him too much; if it did, he didn't speak out about it. Most of the people who spoke out about it were the church members. My father told him to do whatever he thought would make him happy. As his family, we were all pleased about it and accepted his decision."

Sam knew he wanted to be more than just another singer. In fact, he *had* to be more than just another singer. Since the line was so definitively drawn between the two styles, Sam knew that once he went Pop, chances were he could never go back to Gospel. This was an all-or-nothing venture and Sam was leaving a field he had mastered only to become a neophyte once again. In order to go from being a big fish in a small pond to a big fish in a big pond, Sam knew he had to find the secret to mass appeal.

I once asked Charles if Sam had any Pop influences. When I asked "Sam knew what kind of Pop star he wanted to be. Was there anyone in the industry he looked up to or highly regarded?" I got an interesting response. "I'll tell you who he liked." Charles paused, causing me to shift to the edge of my seat. "Elvis Presley. He always did give Elvis his propers. He told people 'that boy's gonna be something else. Any time an entertainer can come off of a layoff like he did (referring to Elvis' 1958-1960 Army stint), follow Sammy Davis, Jr. on a show, and *still* tear up the house, that's a bad man!' He said, 'Y'all watch out for him, that boy is bad!'"

Later in life, Elvis and Sam respectively would become the top two Pop artists for RCA. "They knew one another and had respect for each other," Charles recalls. "There wasn't no "hanging out" or anything like that, but they knew each other, and Sam had a lot of respect for Elvis." Charles also explained Sam recognized all forms of good music, and gave credit where it was due. He held Frank Sinatra in highest regards, feeling that there were only a few people that had the complete singer/performer package, and Sinatra was the best of them all. Sam was in awe of how Sinatra controlled his voice, as well as his ability to work a crowd in a live performance. Charles said Sam also predicted huge success for The Beatles even before the British invasion hit American shores.

Sam strived for both the success and mass appeal Elvis Presley, Frank Sinatra, and The Beatles enjoyed, yet as a black man in America, his approach had to be different. He realized he had to find a way to capture a good share of the white audience while maintaining his black fan base. Sam never did anything haphazardly and since this move was easily the biggest of his career, a lot of forethought went into its execution. He was fascinated with artists who had had previous crossover success—Nat King Cole, Louis Armstrong, Harry Belafonte, and Sammy Davis, Jr. just to name a few. He noted the proclivity of white artists to cover black music, and was intrigued by the amount of success they had. He intensely studied music trends; who was buying what and why? It was here he discovered his strength—the same teenage girls who'd come to Gospel programs to hear him sing about the Lord would undoubtedly come to Pop concerts to hear him sing about love.

In January of 1957, Specialty released Sam's first single, "Lovable," under the fictitious name "Dale Cook." A rework of his gospel hit "He's So Wonderful" with the Soul Stirrers, Sam fooled no one with his alias.

"It was funny to me because I said 'he can't disguise his voice. I don't know why he'd change his name!'" Agnes remembers. "He was kind of reluctant because he didn't know whether the people were going to accept him in Pop or not. Overall, most people finally came around to accept the fact he had moved over. It was a smooth transition."

David tended to agree, adding "It was never a loss of soul. I think that's the main thing. Sam had a 'feeling' he portrayed in his songs. He had smoothness but could also be spiritual. Even his pop songs had a spiritual feeling I don't think anyone else can duplicate. I'm not just saying this because he's my brother and I've admired him all my life, I feel it. The way he'd phrase words, the way he manipulated notes. He was an innovative and very unique artist."

The song, intended to woo the teenage market, missed its mark. While I agree with my uncle's statement about Sam's Pop songs having a spiritual nature, I don't feel it applies to this record. I'm a big fan of "Wonderful" but I'm not crazy about "Lovable," not only because the song sounds remanufactured, but because Sam fails to bring the same passion as in the original. Sam replaces the subject in the song: "God" goes from being "wonderful" to "my girl" being "so lovable" and the song loses all of its spiritual feeling. The background singers chant *lovable* in a monotone manner that's stiff and irritating, effectively canceling out Sam's smooth, carefree delivery. As a result, the earth-moving Gospel song that was "Wonderful" translates to nothing but an uninspired Pop song.

While "Lovable" came up short of its desired result, the record was not a total flop. "Lovable" had enough impact to let the world know that Sam Cook was no longer a Gospel singer, but a true Pop convert. What seemed a good beginning, however, turned out to be the end—at least as far Specialty Records was concerned.

After a stormy disagreement with owner Art Rupe, Sam, along with his producer Robert "Bumps" Blackwell, bolted Specialty for a start-up label called Keen Records. It seems Rupe wasn't too crazy about Bumps' unconventional recording session in which Sam used white background singers, and dared the producer to try and make a hit record with his present arrangement. What Rupe didn't realize was that Sam and Bumps had a plan: they figured that in order to reel in the white audience, Sam's songs would have to combine his sultry voice with a less "intimidating" background. Rupe told Bumps he'd trade Sam's demo tapes for royalties

Bumps had coming from Specialty, estimated at some $50,000. Bumps accepted the challenge and pursuant to their separation agreement, the pair walked out of Specialty's doors with a set of Sam's demo tapes. The master tapes included a remake of George Gershwin's "Summertime" from the hit play *Porgy and Bess,* as well as a song Sam had written himself: a repetitive little number they'd use as a B-side and call "You Send Me."

Some of history's greatest discoveries were purely accidental. In the 17th century, Isaac Newton was inspired to formulate his complex proof of gravity by walking through an orchard and seeing an apple fall from a tree. In 1929, a London scientist with an unsanitary laboratory returned from vacation and was shocked to see that mold had grown in one of his Petri dishes and had killed the bacteria sample inside. Dr. Alexander Fleming's lack of cleanliness had accidentally led to the discovery of Penicillin. Bubble gum, x-rays, Velcro, TNT, even Post-It notes, were all discovered by accident.

The work of art that is "You Send Me" was no accident. It was intentionally armed with a catchy hook, a simple melody, and a couple of well-placed *whoa-ohs* that Sam was famous for in gospel and now established as his pop trademark. It possessed the spiritual smoothness David had alluded to earlier by introducing an innovative blend of Gospel, R&B and Pop. It was written for the young teenaged female just like his first release, but where "Lovable" missed the mark, "You Send Me" hit its intended target right straight square in the heart.

What *was* an accident was the discovery of Sam's hidden gem. Sam and Bumps were just as surprised as the rest of America when the song started to take off nationally. The pair had been aiming for crossover success, but "You Send Me" turned out to be a hit on black radio first. It wasn't until a Detroit DJ named Casey Kasem started playing "You Send Me" did the record catch on in white markets.

Also important to note is the fact that the song's potential was miscalculated not just by one recording expert—but two. Art Rupe first let the song walk out the door in a fit of anger. Then Bumps Blackwell, despite being desperate to come up with a hit, dismissed the song as B-side material and let it sit on the shelf for four months before releasing it.

By now, Dale Cook was no more. "Lovable" made just enough of a splash for the gospel world to realize their Dove had taken flight, so he didn't have much of a choice but to go forward using his real first name. In addition, he adopted a mark of distinction that would separate his gospel past from his secular future. From this point on he would be known to the world as Sam Cooke.

"My mother said Sam added the "e" to his name because of superstition of names ending with "k" in show business," Hattie's daughter, Doncella, explains. "It was thought that tragic things, bad luck things would happen to you. Adding the "e" did not change the pronunciation of the name; it was still pronounced "Cook." Dionne Warwicke at one time did the same thing."

"Summertime" was released by Sam Cooke with high expectations in September of 1957. The A-side is one of my personal favorites, but it barely registered a blip on the Pop chart—peaking at #81 after four weeks—as word spread quickly that the home run was the flipside. "You Send Me" would go to #1 on both the Pop and R & B charts, stay on the charts an amazing 26 weeks, and eventually sell over 1.7 million singles. Sam Cooke, in his quest for a breakout record, had quickly become the latest pop sensation.

"To me it was a proud feeling," Agnes recalls. "The record was going over so big, everywhere you went, people were playing it. All the neighbors were talking about it. When you walked down the street in our neighborhood that's all you heard coming out of people's windows playing over and over again. Back then, neighborhoods were like family. Everybody knew everybody and everybody loved Sam. They were truly happy for him."

"Man, the stores had a run on that song that was really something else!" Charles' eyes beamed as he relived the memory. "The song was everywhere, all over. It definitely went beyond Sam's expectations. As a matter of fact it went beyond everyone's expectations."

As "You Send Me" was climbing up the charts nationally, interesting developments were taking place behind the scenes that would later help define Sam's unique status as an artist. One of the conditions of Sam's separation from Specialty was that all publishing rights to the songs he had written under contract were to remain the property of Art Rupe's Venice Music Publishing. This created a bitter disagreement between Rupe and Keen's founders, Bob Keane and John Siamas. The Keen founders quickly responded by copywriting "You Send Me" with Sam's brother L.C. as writer, thereby side-stepping Sam's agreement with Specialty. They later did the same with several other songs in dispute so that Keen's publishing company could control those as well. Accusations flew, lawyers were summoned, and Sam himself was brought into the middle of the scuffle with a personal letter from Art Rupe begging him to admit the song's publishing actually belonged to Venice. The whole time Sam sat back like a young child listening to a racy adult conversation, soaking the information in and filing it away for future reference. He saw that these men understood there was something very important about the ownership of his publishing rights: money. He began to wonder why *he* wasn't the owner of his copyrights. After all, didn't he write the songs in question? Why was he letting others argue over what should rightfully be his?

In the meantime, Art Rupe realized he had made a huge mistake the day he let Sam and "You Send Me" walk away from Specialty Records, but nevertheless saw the golden opportunity that lay ahead. Not letting his ego get the best of him, he rummaged through studio demo tapes to see if he could duplicate the success of "You Send Me." What he found was a demo of "I'll Come Running Back to You," complete with Sam's guitar accompaniment. Confident he could cook up a hit with the similar recipe, he summoned the same white background singers he threatened to expel from the "You Send Me" session, as well as the session's arranger, Rene Hall. "I'll Come Running Back to You," released just two months after "You Send Me," would soar to #18 Pop and #1 R&B, giving Sam his second million-selling single of 1957.

Sam had another important business matter he needed to address. Now that he had two breakout singles to promote, he needed his business mentor more than ever. With a promise of financial security, Sam managed to coax S.R. Crain away from the Soul Stirrers and into the

Sam Cooke camp. As Sam's Road Manager, Crain would be in charge of salaries, concert bookings, hotel reservations and expenses. When Sam had a concert, Crain would collect half the money up front, then the other half at intermission or between shows. More importantly, Crain's most valuable asset was that he was someone Sam could trust.

After securing Crain's services, Sam also signed a deal with the prestigious William Morris Agency. Their promise to him (through Bumps, who had also assumed the role of Sam's manager) was a spot on *The Ed Sullivan Show* as well as a run at the granddaddy of all supper clubs, New York City's Copacabana.

Everything in Sam's life was moving at break-neck speed. He spent 1956 as a disgruntled member of the nation's top gospel group with no clear-cut plan to cure his unhappiness in sight. By the end of 1957 he had gone from Sam Cook to Dale Cook to Sam Cooke and had two #1 solo singles—as a *pop* star. "You Send Me" had already saturated black airwaves and was starting to have the same affect on white radio. In addition, WMA made good on its promise of delivering *The Ed Sullivan Show*. His prime-time appearance on *Ed Sullivan* in November of 1957 would introduce him to millions of American families, and the handsome, well-groomed singer was sure to make a killing on a national level. Sam had a feeling he was on the road to stardom and he was right–he just had no idea how bumpy the road ahead would actually be.

Because he was a new artist, Sam was the last scheduled act on the show. Ed Sullivan gave him a gracious introduction and the crowd responded accordingly, eagerly waiting to attach a face and figure to the hot pop song. Sam attacked "You Send Me" with amazing confidence, but never made it out of the opening verse of the song before the screen switched to the CBS trademark logo; his national debut had been clipped short due to network time constraints. Initially this had to be a major embarrassment for Sam, but the next turn of events would alleviate any doubts about his mainstream acceptance: thousands of angry fans bombarded the show with letters and phone calls demanding his time be reinstated. The following week, Sam was rescheduled and sang not only "You Send Me," but his next Keen release, "(I Love You) For Sentimental Reasons" as well. Sam did make a killing on a national level, it just took a little longer than he imagined. In that short span however, sales of "You Send Me" soared as America awaited Sam Cooke's proper introduction.

The Copacabana, on the other hand, started off as a nightmare and got progressively worse. Famous for its tuxedoed waiters, world-class cuisine, and high-society clientele, the Copa was considered New York City's most prestigious supper club. It was located on the city's East Side on the corner of 60th Street and Fifth Avenue, and by 1958 had hosted the likes of Martin and Lewis, Frank Sinatra, Nat King Cole, Billy Eckstine, and Tony Bennett. Sam now had a chance to leave his mark on the same stage as such music and comedy legends, but the mark he would leave would be anything but memorable.

In March of 1958, Sam started his three-week engagement on the wrong foot and never regained his balance. A large part of Sam's problem had to do with the act's preparation. Having abandoned their recent hits for ballads and classic show tunes, Bumps Blackwell neglected to rewrite Sam's arrangements to accommodate an orchestra, and then miscalculated how large the orchestra itself would be. Instead of having a polished, rehearsed act, Bumps and Rene Hall had to hustle to complete the forgotten parts of the arrangements up until the time the curtain opened.

Another part of the problem was Sam's lack of nightclub experience and stage presence. Bumps hired a choreographer to teach the rhythm-challenged singer some soft-shoe dance steps at the last minute. He brought in a costume designer that dressed him up to be more "cute" than Cooke. Sam had to be rehearsed on basics like body language—he wasn't quite sure how to stand or what to do with his hands—and as a result, his stage presence seemed awkward and his delivery unconvincing. Part of Sam's pop routine involved talking to the audience between songs, using his charming personality to get comfortable with the crowd. But he had nothing in common with the mostly middle-aged, Jewish audience and would have embarrassing moments of silence and break out into cold sweats. Sam did sing "You Send Me," but ignored other pop hits within his realm. He instead opted for more obscure songs in his repertoire like "Canadian Sunset" and "Begin the Beguine." At several points in the show he and the orchestra were miles apart, and the cold sweats and periods of silence would reappear. It was evident that Sam Cooke and Bumps Blackwell were ill-prepared for the culture shock the Copacabana provided. In fact, one could say they were in well over their heads.

It didn't help that Sam was the opening act for the veteran Jewish comedian Myron Cohen. The crowd was clearly there to see him, and Cohen took advantage of that fact to rip Sam's performance throughout his show. Magazine reviews hinted that Sam Cooke was better suited as a teen idol (even though he had just turned 27), and that he wasn't quite ready for more sophisticated venues. Sam was stunned by his 1958 failure at the Copa, and the experience would haunt him for several years to come. Over the course of time, he would realize he tried to give the crowd what he thought they wanted to see and hear instead of an act *he* was comfortable delivering. Sam wouldn't get the chance to redeem himself for another six and a half years, but once he did, his 1964 return engagement would be one of the most triumphant accomplishments of his stellar career. "Sam Cooke at the Copa" would symbolize a fresh new direction the singer had in mind, and would reinforce his status as one of the most versatile entertainers ever to take stage. It would also mark the last live album he'd ever record.

Chapter Five

Uncle Sam and the Family

GWEN SIGHED AS THE SPORTS car pulled away from the red, white and blue arched entrance of Riverview Amusement Park. Slightly nauseated and thoroughly fatigued, Gwen now regretted eating that last ice cream bar before riding the "Strat-O-Stat" swing ride. She angled Sam's rear view mirror to see her younger cousins Gene, 13, Renee, 10, and Maurice, 15, quietly nestled in the car's back seat and knew within minutes they'd all be asleep. It was a warm July night, 1963, and she enjoyed the annual outing with her Uncle Sam at age 18 as much as she did when she was 12.

Riverview Park is legendary in Chicago's history. Billed as the world's largest amusement park in its time, it sat on the city's predominantly white Northwest side. The park was bordered by Lane Tech H.S. on the north, Belmont Avenue on the south, Western Avenue on the east, and the Chicago River on the west, hence the name "Riverview." The 140-acre park was the home of "The Bobs," America's fastest rollercoaster, and "The Fireball," a coaster which featured a dip that went through an underground tunnel. Its oldest attraction was the "Shoot-the-Chutes" water ride, and the walk-through fun house "Aladdin's Castle" featured a giant-sized, turbaned Aladdin's head mounted at the entrance to an Arabian "city."

Once a year, Sam would make a point to take his nieces and nephews, affectionately nicknamed the "Gashouse Gang," to Riverview for a day of all-out, unbridled hedonism. "Anything goes" was the motto of the day when Sam took his family to Riverview: hot dogs, sno-cones, sodas, ice cream, and cotton candy were on an all-you-can-eat basis, and the kids rarely got cheated. Riverview Park had a small admission charge and tickets were bought individually at a typical cost of $.25-.45 each.

For a young black girl growing up on Chicago's South side, these

Riverview outings represented Heaven on earth. Nothing was too good or too much on this day. "When our parents would take us to Riverview, we would be limited on the number of rides we could ride because you'd have to pay individually," Gwen recalls. "But when Sam took you, there were no holds barred! Sam would give the ticket attendant a $50 bill and tell them 'let them ride as many times as they want!'"

Aladdin's Castle Fun House at Riverview Park.

(Courtesy of Chuck Wlodarczyk of Riverview Publications)

In years past, Sam would pack the kids into his limousine, but today, at Gwen's request, they rode in Sam's convertible Ferrari. Midnight blue with blue leather interior, Gwen remembered the car's soft top was custom-made of blue denim, complete with dark blue stitching. "The top actually looked like a worn pair of blue jeans," she would recall. "I told Sam we just *had* to ride in this car today!" And so it was.

As the oldest she got to ride in the front seat with her cousins occupying the Ferrari's limited back seat. Accompanying them to the park in the limo directly behind them were Sam's good friends, actor Brock Peters and singer Nancy Wilson. In reflection, Gene would say "Nancy had a huge crush on Sam back then, everyone could see it. But Sam labeled her as a 'good girl' and wouldn't approach her, out of respect." Brother David, "Gashousers" Toni, Donald, Ophelia, and Doncella, and daughter Linda were in still another limousine. The convoy, two limousines trailing a convertible Ferrari, had to be a sight to behold traveling northbound on the newly-constructed Dan Ryan Expressway.

This type of outing was typical of Sam's nature. When describing Sam Cook the person, his never-ending generosity was one of his most prominent characteristics. To his family and friends money was never an object, and Sam always requested the best of everything. In the summer of 1961, for example, Sam was booked for a run at Detroit's Flame Show Bar. The entourage of friends and family making the trip from Chicago was so large that Sam bought out the entire floor of a local hotel just so his guests wouldn't be disturbed.

"We were too young to go to the show and had to stay at the hotel," Gene remembers, "but me and Maurice had our own room. Sam told us if we picked up the phone and ordered room service, they'd bring us anything we needed. Maurice and I ordered cheeseburgers, french fries, milkshakes… more food than *three* kids could possibly eat! The hotel TV's were on timers–I think a half hour was 25 cents–so Sam left us with a bag full of quarters. We fed the TV all night long. Even after we had dozed off, if I woke up, I'd put another quarter in, if Maurice woke up, he'd put more quarters in. Between us, we managed to keep it on all night long!"

Sam with his friend Eunice, 1956. Sam is holding his newborn niece, Toni.

(*Photos courtesy of Toni Cook Howard*)

Sometimes during his visits, Sam would spoil his nieces and nephews not with money, but with his time and attention. "The memories I have are from our July picnics," L.C.'s daughter Toni remarks. "When someone would approach him, he would be nice to his fans, but you couldn't take him away from his purpose for being there. He would acknowledge them but then say 'Excuse me. I'm with my niece now.' So we never felt like he pushed us to the side because of his fans. Those days were his family days."

"During one of our picnics, however, word quickly spread throughout the park Sam Cooke was there. Of course, some couldn't believe that it was really him so they came over and asked him 'are you really Sam Cooke?' Sam responded with a big smile. He invited his fans to be a part of his dance contest. Somebody put "Twistin' the Night Away" on the portable record player and Sam sang along with the record while we were all twisting. It wasn't about finding a winner; it was all about having a good time.

Everyone, young and old, twisted on the makeshift dance floor. When the contest was over, Sam thanked everyone and told them that he wanted to spend time with his family, and when he did that I couldn't help but thinking what a neat person my uncle was. He managed to make that day a special day for his fans, but he also made his family feel like we were the most important people in his world."

Scenes from the Cook family picnic, July 1962: a) Mary and Agnes working the grill. b) The family doing a dance called "The Madison". c) The adults playing cards.

The "Gashouse Gang," 1962. Top row: Maurice (in batter's stance), Gene (with ball),
Donald, Doncella. Bottom row: Renee, Ophelia, and Toni.

(Photos courtesy of Toni Cook Howard)

"It used to be a lot of fun when he came home because we (the kids) had
our day with him, no matter what," Agnes' daughter Renee recalls. "It was
our day to do whatever we wanted to do. Our parents were not allowed to
come with us; it was just us. And then we had our own individual days. I
remember one time he came to my mother's house with his limousine and
he said 'C'mon, I'm going to take you for a ride. Bring all your friends!' I
said 'I don't want all my friends in here!' Then he said, 'Tell you what. I'll
chauffeur you anywhere you want to go. Tell me where you want to go.' So

we drove around the neighborhood and I waved to my little friends. Some asked 'can I get in?' and I let them in, and he took us wherever we wanted to go. This was just Sam, and we enjoyed that time with him."

Renee's older brother Gene remembers the practical jokes Sam used to play:

"One time Sam and Charles took me to the main little spot where everyone hung out. Everyone was looking at this limousine pulling up slowly, and I rolled the window down. 'Hey! That's Gene!' So Sam gets out of the car and he's talking to everybody and signing autographs. One of the young guys in the neighborhood says 'Mr. Cooke, you left your lights on.' Sam says, 'Gene, you didn't tell them about the lights?' We all knew to follow along. 'Naw, Sam, you told me not to tell them!' Sam says 'I wave my hand and my lights go out. As a matter of fact, my brother can wave his hand and make the lights go out.' Uncle Charlie (gave the cue), and the lights went out. Needless to say, this was one the first cars with sentinel lights, or as they call them now, delayed headlights. When I got to school that Monday, the whole playground was waiting for me. 'Man, would you tell them Sam Cooke has lights in his limousine, that when he waves his hands, the lights go off?' My uncles had it timed so perfectly."

Sam also made a point to be home for Thanksgiving. Mama Cook had a tradition of having family picnics in July and she insisted all her children come home every November. "I vividly remember the holidays, because we always had good times," Agnes recalls. "He'd always make sure he didn't have engagements during Thanksgiving, because he knew he had to come home."

"But remember, he didn't eat for two or three days!" David chimed in, causing everyone to break out in laughter.

"He wanted to be able to enjoy everything my mom cooked, so he would fast the day before," Agnes explained. "And, man, could he eat! To be such a small man, he could really eat!"

My mother remembers Christmas vacation 1959, when she, my grandmother, and her brother Donald drove to California to visit Sam and Barbara:

"I was 14½ the time we drove from Chicago to Los Angeles to visit my Uncle Sam and Aunt Barbara. Boy was it a long drive! I remember thinking I had never heard so much Country Western music on the radio in all my life! This was my first trip to the west coast. In fact it was unique in that I enjoyed a lot of "first" experiences. For example, having never really been out of Chicago, it marked the first time I stayed in a hotel."

"By the time we arrived in Los Angeles, I felt as if I were in another world. As we entered the city, I was in awe of the palm trees lining the streets and neighborhoods instead of the familiar maple trees I was used to in Chicago."

"Sam and Barbara lived in an apartment, and when we arrived, Barbara prepared a Porterhouse steak with all the trimmings, my *first* steak dinner. After we ate, Sam convinced my mother that I was old enough to sit with the adults and have after-dinner wine. As we sat on the floor around a large round coffee table, Sam brought out a small decanter of warm liquid and tiny ceramic cups with no handles. He said he was introducing us to the art of drinking Sake, reminding us to only take small sips each time. Needless to say, this led to my first experience of being totally smashed!"

"After returning to the hotel and going to bed, every time I tried to close my eyes, the room would spin. I was so frightened and did not understand what was happening to me, I started yelling for my mother. She brought me a cold towel and stayed to comfort me until I fell asleep."

"The next day, when Mother told Sam and Barbara what had happened, everybody laughed, everybody except me of course. Looking back, this is probably why I shied away from drinking until I was a *real* adult."

"I quickly sobered up, however, when Sam announced the agenda for the day. He was taking us all to Disneyland. This was beyond my wildest dreams. To me, I saw this as rich people's Riverview. I just knew I had skyrocketed to another planet! As I look back, I think my Uncle Sam was as charged up as I was about amusement parks. This may explain why I love amusement parks as much as I do today. Taking the children is just an excuse to get there as far as I'm concerned!"

Disneyland, December, 1959. Top row, Barbara, Sam, Mary and a family friend. Bottom row, Sam's nephew Donald and daughter Linda. Niece Gwendolyn took the picture.

(Photo courtesy of Donald Miller)

"I don't know if they had just moved to this apartment or not," my uncle Donald, in a separate interview, remembers about this same visit. "But upon arrival, I took a bath. I must have been 8 or 9 years old."

"You were only 5, Donald," my mother interjects, reminding him as only a big sister could. Actually Donald was six years old at the time.

"Anyway, I went to turn on the water and it came out brown with rust. I didn't know any better, so I just started hollering at the top of my lungs. 'Mama! Come get me!' She came in the bathroom 'What's wrong?' 'There's something wrong with these people's water! Get me outta here! I wanna go home!' My mother said 'It's just a little rust, calm down.' I said 'These people are po', Mama! Take me back home!'"

"Well, the next time we went back to Los Angeles, it was a completely different scenario." Donald slowly and methodically recalls the differences. "Sam had a mansion. We rode in a Bentley. The water was crystal. And I was ashamed to sit down on the toilet seat because it was inlaid with silver dollar coins. I looked around and said 'we can stick around here a little while, Mama. They've picked things up a bit!'"

Besides these rare road trips and the annual July and Thanksgiving visits, there were times when Sam's tour schedule would naturally bring him back through the Windy City. Just because Sam was working, however, didn't mean he didn't spend time with his family. Quite often, his dressing room would be packed with his relatives, including the infamous "Gashouse Gang."

"The Regal was <u>the</u> theatre for black performers in Chicago," Doncella says proudly. "Whenever Sam performed, we went. Sometimes we'd go every day the show was going on. The people knew us backstage. We'd knock on the door, Sam would let us in, and we'd stay. Sometimes they'd have to tell Sam 'time for you to change', because he'd be back there spending time with us. Other performers would come in and say 'hi', but Sam's time was mostly spent with us."

It was during these local stops Sam and Maurice would engage in their checker wars. When Sam came to town and they didn't have any checkers, he'd send someone to the store to get a checkerboard. Maurice was good at checkers, but Sam would constantly talk while the game was going on to try and break Maurice's concentration.

"Backstage at the Regal when the guy came and told Sam 'you're on', Sam would always tell Maurice 'Gotta go to work!'" my mother remembers. "They'd stop the game and come back to it when he was done. They did this for years."

"Sam would play against Maurice, and Gene was Maurice's coach," Doncella adds. He would always tell Maurice 'Don't listen to Sam. Don't let him talk you out of your game.'"

"Because he would!" Gene says emphatically. "Sam would say 'Man, we just got off tour, and they brought 10 dudes to the hotel to play me, and I whipped them all.' Maurice would say 'Really, Sam?' We would get to listening to Sam's story, next thing you know Sam would have three more kings! So I'd say 'Don't listen to him, Reece!'"

Sam would always find some sort of competition for the Gashouse Gang, and it usually involved pitting the girls against the boys. A softy at heart, he always found a way to tilt the odds in favor of the girls.

"We would have battles when Sam came to town; the boys against the girls," Gene remembers. "The boys would <u>never</u> win! I must admit, the girls would work a couple of days before we would. We would start the last day. But Sam was partial to the girls and he helped them along, showing them little steps, saying 'you hit this note, and you hit that one.' They used to kick our butts every time!"

"Gwen was the leader of the girls and David was the leader of the boys," Doncella adds. "We'd have our competitions, and we <u>knew</u> we were good! One time we made up a dance (routine) to Baby Washington's "Leave Me Alone." It just so happened, the next time Sam came to town, she was in the lineup. We knew Sam was the boss, so we went to him and said 'you know we made up this dance to "Leave Me Alone." Can we go on stage? We could be her background dancers!' My sister Ophelia and my cousins Renee and Cookie were like 7 or 8. I was about 10. It made no difference they were professionals, and forget about the backup singers she already had, we were good!"

"Because he *told* us we were good!" Ophelia kicks in.

"Sam didn't want to hurt our feelings, so he told us how she had her own professional dancers, but that we could dance with him," Doncella continues. "That's one reason Ophelia ended up on stage with him doing the twist." Ophelia is the little girl pictured twisting with Sam on stage in the liner notes to "The Man and His Music."

"I <u>begged</u> him!" Ophelia cried. "I remember sitting on his lap playing with his hair, rubbing his face and saying 'but you said we were good! Pleeease can we go on stage and dance with Baby Washington?' He kept saying 'a little more practice, baby, a little more practice.' Then he told us 'I could book you in Philly for $25 a week' and we said '$25 a week? That's not enough money!' Granted, we were only 7 years old at the time!"

"He would have us escorted from the back stage of the Regal down to the front, so we could sit in the front row. In every one of his shows he would pick people from the audience to come on stage and dance with him. Of course I was right there… (she waves her arms frantically). Never did I realize how important that moment would be to me. I didn't get paid, but I was there!"

Sam would often introduce the Gashouse Gang to the other entertainers on the Regal show bill, but there were certain entertainers that were off limits. For example, he made it a point to distance the kids from the Temptations, mainly because of David Ruffin's well-publicized drug abuse. Sam had a bitter disgust for drugs but instead of passing judgment, he simply separated himself and his family from such entertainers and their illicit activities. "He would tell us 'you can't go up to that person,'" Renee recalls. "And we would say 'why not?' We found out later it was because of the things they were doing." There were also entertainers who had an eye for young girls, and Sam shielded his nieces from them as well. "There were only certain entertainers we were allowed to be around by ourselves," Renee continues. "As we got older, we understood why."

Riverview Park, July 1962. Back row: Maurice, Gene, and Doncella.
Front row: Toni and Ophelia.

(Photo courtesy of Toni Cook Howard)

Charles' daughter Charlene (we've always called her "Cookie"), was actually lucky enough to go out on the road with Sam and her father. When she was 7 or 8 she was supposed to spend the summer with her father, but he was preparing to hit the road with Sam. When she found out she was going to have to stay with relatives while her father worked, she was sad, but my grandmother had a plan. "My aunt Mary told me 'Just cry, he won't leave you, just cry'. So, of course when it got time for him to go out on the road with Sam, I cried. I had the unique experience of spending two weeks on the road with them. They didn't travel back then like they do now, tour busses and all. I had to sit in the car while they performed, but I remember the thrill of being out there on the road with them like it was yesterday."

As a young boy of 4 or 5, some of the first Sam Cooke stories I consciously recall were of how my mother cherished the moments Sam came home to Chicago. I distinctly remember one of these stories because her eyes would begin to tear as she told it, and until she talked of Sam I had never seen her cry. At that age it was quite traumatic to see someone as bubbly and as full of life as my mother, someone I relied on for strength, weaken as she talked about her late uncle, and pretty soon my face was full of tears, too. She dried my eyes and explained to me that tears were not always painful; that sometimes people cried tears of pleasure. Although this made no sense to me at the time, I was comforted by the fact that she could indeed smile as she remembered the past:

"Those times when Sam would come to town, we would do things like go to Riverview during the day, but in the evening we would all gather back at my grandma's house. She'd have food cooked, we'd eat, and then we would all sit around on the floor. Sam would make up stories, make up songs, and we'd play competitive games—boys against the girls. David and I are close in age, and although he was our uncle, he would take the boys. Sam would always make us compete. Who could do "this" the best? Who could do "that" the best? Who could remember things he had told us before? Who could recite that poem, sing that song he had taught us the year before? These were all ad lib things; he wouldn't have anything planned. He would just come up with a story or a song and it was up to you to remember that the next time."

"We would all sit in a circle and Sam would just—'la dee da dee da'—make up a song on the spot. He would assign parts to everybody. I will never, ever, forget. Back then, Cowboys and Indians were really popular. He started beating (she starts a rhythmic "drumbeat" on the table) and then he said:

Out of the lodge, at even tide
Across the sleepy lagoon
Indian maiden by his side,
The Indian maiden Pale Moon.

All the Indians dancing 'round
The teepees late at night
Except the one who's mooning 'round
The one who lost the fight.

They fought for the Indian maid
To see who'd marry soon
One brave was the lucky one
He won little Pale Moon.

Now they come out of the lodge at even tide
Across the sleepy lagoon
Indian maiden by his side
The Indian maiden Pale Moon
The Indian maiden Pale Moon…" (fades out as beating stops)

"I remember every last word. He did it one year, one time. And made up the words on the spot, he definitely did. I took every last word in and I remembered it. I'm 58 years old now, and I was a little girl, so this has been with me all my life. Do you see what an impression my uncle had on me? For him to sit up there and make up a song for us, it was left up to me to remember that. It was an impromptu thing, nothing planned. He would just make it up right there on the spot. And that's what impressed us the most. We had an uncle that could do anything. He was like a God as far as we were concerned."

I hadn't heard my mother sing that song in years before that testimony. It brought back memories for me because she would often sing it as a lullaby. My mother has always had a smooth and soothing voice, one perfect for storytelling. As a kindergarten teacher, the children she has in her classroom are blessed, because her voice makes for powerful visualizations during story time. At bedtime, she would also sing Sam's version of "Summertime," and I was almost grown before I realized Sam recorded it. Then when I heard Sam's version of "Summertime," it brought back the most comforting memories of my childhood, memories in which my mother would sing me to sleep.

Chapter Six

From Tribulation to Triumph: Sam Takes Control of his Career

IN NOVEMBER OF 1958, WHILE driving to Mississippi from a show in St. Louis, Sam was involved in a serious car accident. Sam, Lou Rawls, guitarist Clif White, and Sam's driver, Eddie Cunningham, were driving at night on an unlit stretch of Highway 61 in Arkansas. As they were coming over a hill, they spotted a truck that was parked in their lane, but it was too late to stop. "Sam told Eddie 'hit the ditch!'" Charles recollects. "Eddie tried, but couldn't do it." The convertible Cadillac, traveling almost 140 m.p.h., rammed full speed into the back of the truck, shearing off the convertible's top and windshield on impact and lodging the car beneath the truck's bed.

David was just seventeen at the time, but had been with Sam the night before. He remembered "It was about a year after "You Send Me" had hit. Sam was in St. Louis playing the Sportsman's Club and staying at the Atlas Hotel. Sam had flown to St. Louis and Eddie had driven me from Chicago by car. I had been hanging with Sam and the fellas—Lou Rawls and J.W. Alexander were there with the Pilgrim Travelers,..."

"They were The Travelers by then," Charles interrupts. "They had changed their name from The Pilgrim Travelers to just The Travelers. The first time I met Eddie I said 'man, you drive too fast.' But I've got to give it to Eddie. Eddie took him a job. Sam had a white leather coat that had gotten dirty. Eddie went out and got some saddle soap while Sam was on stage and cleaned Sam's coat so well, Sam didn't even recognize his own coat! Eddie was a valet from the beginning. He would press Sam's pants, help him with his coat; Sam told Crain 'hire this man!'"

"That night, Eddie took me to the airport," David continued. "That was the first plane ride I'd ever had. Papa picked me up from the airport that night. The next morning, I found out Sam had the accident. Sam was lucky though. All he got was just some pieces of glass in his eye."

"Yeah, Eddie drove fast," Charles said, shaking his head at the tragedy of the accident. "He hit the back end of that truck full speed. Every time I rode with him, I told him 'man, you drive much too fast.'"

Sam was in the hospital for a few days, but was emotionally shaken from the accident for some time to come. Lou Rawls was in a coma for five days and Clifton White broke his collarbone. Eddie Cunningham died from his accident injuries. It was then Sam hired his older brother, Charles, as his full time driver. Charles toured with Sam for the rest of his pop career, and as a result of his experiences with Sam, is an integral part of this book.

I made the statement earlier that sometimes we have to be "blessed" with tragedy in order to grow as human beings. While the violent manner in which Eddie Cunningham lost his life was certainly tragic, it brought Sam and Charles closer than they'd ever been. Charles missed three of Sam's formative years serving in the military, so these times were special in establishing the great bond they'd share as both brothers and friends. The Cooks raised their children to believe that there was nothing more important in life than family and as Charles relives times spent on the road with Sam, I can tell he truly admired his famous younger brother.

Sam and Charles with Charles' mother-in-law, Mary Johnson.

(Photo courtesy of Martin Cook)

Remembering the difficult conditions Sam experienced while he was on the road as a gospel singer—second class meals, limited hotels, etc.— I asked Charles was life on the road tough after Sam went pop.

"Not for me it wasn't. Every week I'd get $1000 for expenses. Then if I had $400 left, which I never did (he laughs)...he'd give me six (hundred) more to make up the difference. Sam told me 'if we're ever in jail and can't get out...man, don't ever be caught without enough money to get out of jail.'" Touring the country at a time when police could arrest blacks for little to no reason at all, it was important to always be prepared for whatever may happen.

"Muhammad Ali would meet us out there on the road sometimes," Charles continued. "Sam and Ali were good friends. Ali always wanted to hang with Sam. He would call Sam and find out his tour schedule, then catch up with us in different cities."

I learned a lot about Sam's nuances from things that happened on the road. Wherever Sam went, for example, he would always have his Road Manager S.R. Crain carry his briefcase. While the briefcase may not have been out of the ordinary to the casual observer, it in fact contained important papers of a different kind. Checking into a Holiday Inn in Shreveport, Louisiana in 1963, the contents came in handy:

"One time Sam had a Masarati that had a shortage or something in the horn when you turned," David retells the story. "When they went to the hotel the horn went off. The manager came out, going off. Sam said 'man, there's a shortage in the horn, don't talk to me like that.' So the manager called the police."

"The horn stuck and they locked us up saying we were going around blowing our horn because we were refused admittance to the hotel," Charles takes over. Crain had made reservations, but when they arrived, Sam and his band members were told the rooms wouldn't be available for another six hours. "The police came and locked our asses up."

"Charles told the police 'OK then, take me to jail,'" David says, already anticipating the end of the story. "And Crain, you're coming with me. Just bring the briefcase.'"

"We got to the station, the police opened the briefcase up and man… they thought we were bank robbers or something! The briefcase was *full* of money! We'd do one-nighters and get paid every night. When Crain would get paid he'd put the money on in there and keep a running total on his pad."

"And they just paid the bail right out of the briefcase! What was so funny was Charles said 'Crain, you're coming with me!'"

"Because he knew Crain had the money!" Agnes joins in. "They would have this briefcase filled with money, their "money" briefcase. Wherever they went, Sam and Crain used to always have a briefcase full of money because they never knew what was going to happen. He said he may have to get on a plane and he wasn't waiting for nobody to send him some money. Anywhere they went, they always had cash money to do whatever they wanted to do."

"The cops let us go and Crain went on and deducted the bail money off his pad!" Charles notes.

It seems Sam didn't give the briefcase special treatment, and as a result it never raised attention in public circles. "He wouldn't say nothing about it; he'd just lay it down," Agnes' husband Joe Hoskins admits. "But see, nobody knew what was in it."

One of S.R. Crain's duties was to handle Sam's business expenses. In a simplified way, that meant monitoring what went into and what came out of the money briefcase. Sam and Crain had worked closely together since Sam's days with the Soul Stirrers, but there was one time Crain wasn't quite sure how to separate business from friendship in order to handle a particularly delicate situation. Finally, he settled on the direct approach.

"You know, Charlie's been spending a little too much money lately," Crain blurted out, catching Sam off guard. Sam immediately shot a look at Crain. "Let me tell you something and I want you to get this straight. *Anything* he wants, he represents me. That's my brother."

"Crain meant well," David sympathized. "He just picked the wrong person to say they were spending too much money."

Agnes agreed, adding "That's right. Don't *ever* tell Sam 'Charles is spending too much money!'"

Granted, some of the stories Charles tells about life on the road with Sam are best left right there—on the road. But through my uncles, I learned to respect the amount of style, class and professionalism with which Sam ran his career. For one thing, his band members were the best musicians in the industry and Sam respected their talents. "Sam's entourage was the highest paid out there on the road," David said. "*Everybody* wanted to work for Sam. He had top flight people working for him, and he paid them what they were worth. Sam did it with class. He was the first one with a limousine. Sam always had a class act."

Charles surmised it was not only because of Sam's generosity, but that Sam always wanted to surround himself with the best in the business, and didn't mind paying someone if they had a special talent. "He found a barber in New York that cut his hair just the way he liked it. He liked his hair cut with scissors only, never clippers. He always wanted to look professional. Anyway, he paid this guy's way from New York to Cincinnati. He put him up in a hotel for the weekend, but then the guy just had to get back to his shop. Sam understood. Sam sent him home and gave him $500 on top of it. He never hesitated to help the little man out. David was right, Sam always had class."

"On the road he made us (the driver and band members) wear black pants and white shirts when we were traveling," Charles continued. "You had an outfit you had to wear, black pants and a white shirt. We traveled in the limousine and a station wagon." The station wagon, with secured top, carried their luggage and the band's equipment.

"Sam would be in the limo, unless he had some music to go over. Then he'd have Clif, the guitar player, and the drummer (June Gardner) in there with him. Now, if it was over 200 miles or so, Sam wasn't gonna ride in no limousine. Sam would fly and meet us there. But on the road we would walkie-talkie the station wagon from his limo."

Once Charles mentioned the walkie-talkie, it reminded me of something my mother told me years ago, something that seemed more incredible now that I thought about it.

"Sam had a car phone back then, didn't he?" I asked.

"Yeah, he did!" Charles exclaimed, shocked that I was aware of that fact. "As a matter of fact he had three lines! You dialed YJJR to get the operator, and the number was YL5-3306." Now, it was my turn to be shocked—shocked that he remembered the telephone number after all these years.

"And the horn blew when the phone rang and he was out of the car!" David added. "Yeah, Sam did it in style."

"Perils of the Road," circa 1962: Charles changes a rear flat tire on the band's station wagon as L.C. keeps a watchful eye on Charles' son Marty.

(Photo courtesy of Martin Cook)

On the road, Sam and his crew often gambled to pass the time. Every now and then, they'd play poker, but more often than not, they played Craps for money. They would shoot dice between shows or at intermission, and the after-show games would often go late into the night. When Sam gambled with his band members, he felt guilty about taking their money, which irritated his older brother to no end.

"When Sam won money from the fellas, he would end up giving the money back at the end of the night!" Charles said, twisting his face at the memory. "He would always say 'Man, they can't afford to lose this money.' I used to say 'then they shouldn't gamble!' Shoot, we were all grown men. I used to tell him he was crazy for giving them back the money. Sometimes Sam would end up giving them back more money than they lost!"

Sam had a different outlook when he gambled with other artists, however. Sam would often play for high stakes and in these games they'd play for keeps. Once on tour, he played an all-night poker game with Buddy Holly and his band, the Crickets, and walked away several thousand dollars richer. Sam won the Masarati with the faulty horn in a high-stakes game with the singer Eddie Fischer.

I was under the impression Sam constantly toured in order to support his lavish lifestyle. These are excerpts of a conversation at a family gathering in which I addressed that idea:

Agnes: It's just like when Sam would come to Chicago to the Regal, he'd tell Charles 'Charlie, go get the liquor.' He would buy a case of Scotch; a case of gin…Sam would buy cases of liquor. Johnnie (Taylor) and them, Lou Rawls, they were cheap. They wouldn't give you a drink. Sam kept cases in the dressing room. If you came to Sam and wanted a drink, you got it.

Gwen: There was always a party going on in his dressing room. He entertained. That's why people would love to see him coming, because he would spend. It didn't matter.

Erik: Was he ever in over his head? (The *whole* room reacts).

Joe: (laughs as he says 'no').

David: Oh, no. (Laughing) No. Hell no.

Gwen: No, never.

Erik: I thought Sam was on tour 6-8 months out of the year in order to support his lifestyle. I mean, you can still spend more than you make.

David: But that wasn't the case. Let me tell you where Sam really got his business sense from. When he went to the Soul Stirrers, Sam was about 19 or 20, right? These guys were older, they were professionals. They had been in the business for a while. They knew the ins and outs of gospel singing. Sam learned the business firsthand and grew from there.

Agnes: Sam used to take a lot of money under the table, in cash, to keep from paying taxes on it. But by him dying at an early age, it hurt his children because they couldn't get as much Social Security because he hadn't reported all of his earnings.

Erik: So then that's not true?

Charles: Man, let me tell you something. Sam wasn't never in no trouble with money. Not with the Soul Stirrers, either. Everywhere they went they sold out. Sam made money ever since he got out of high school. He was out there on the road because he *wanted* to be out there. When he wanted to rest, he came home. Trust me, I know.

David: I remember the first time I went to Michigan Avenue, the Magnificent Mile. Brooks Brothers! Now, I had never been in no store on Michigan Avenue. But Sam said 'C'mon man, don't worry about a thing. What are you looking at the price tag for? Get what you want.' And man, did we shop! Sam always told me 'I'd rather spend it on you than give it to Uncle Sam!'

Gwen: You know you were talking about 'did he ever run short?' I could not imagine. I *could* not imagine. He was the most generous individual yet it never seemed to run out.

Joe: He was making too much money.

Charles: He bought everyone who worked for him a car. All his band members got a car except his drummer, because he didn't drive.

David: He bought Charles a Wildcat.

Charles: That's right! We went down to the dealership Sam said "go get you a car." I said "which one?" He said, "Any one you want!" I saw the car I wanted, too; grey with a black top, and a floor console. I drove it off the floor. That was a bad mother, too!

Agnes: Do you remember Duck? (Deceased childhood friend Leroy Hoskins).

Erik: Barely, yeah.

Agnes: He put Duck through school. Sam believed in education.

David: Duck turned out to be one of the fastest court stenographers ever…Duck broke the record.

Agnes: Duck had a family and was having problems paying tuition. When it got back to Sam he was struggling to meet his tuition, Sam got upset at Duck for not coming to him first. Sam told him 'man, if you want to go to school that badly, *I'll* pay your tuition!' And he did. That's just the kind of person Sam was…

One of my reasons for writing this book is to clarify public misconceptions about Sam's personal life and professional career. In the process, I gained more insight into the man himself. I knew his family was of utmost priority, and he wasn't afraid to let others know it. I knew his generosity seemed to know no end, which contributed to him being well-liked and well-respected. I didn't know, for example, how much pride Sam took in the way he presented himself and that he demanded the same from the people he employed.

McKie's Disc Jockey Show Lounge, Chicago, circa 1958. Seated l to r are unidentified,
Sam, Sam's date Mary, Leroy "Duck" Hoskins, Duck's wife Ann, Sam's sister Mary,
Sam's brother Charles, Charles' date Clara Alexander, Maude Crain, S.R. Crain, Belle
Farley, and J.J. Farley of the Soul Stirrers.

(Photo courtesy of Gwendolyn Greene)

Sometimes stars tend to live extravagantly to impress others, and quite often a carefree lifestyle is a result of careless spending, but I now see that Sam's situation was different; once Sam reached financial security, he wasn't ashamed of the fact he had enough money to live a comfortable life. In an age when the import car in America was rare, when Cadillac was considered the top-of-the-line luxury car, Sam owned Ferraris, Jaguars and, thanks to Eddie Fisher, Masaratis. The author and historian Lucius Beebe once proclaimed "All I want is the best of everything," and that central theme seemed to ring true for the way Sam Cooke lived his life.

In November of 1958 he hadn't reached that level of financial security he would one day enjoy, and it was during this period he realized something had to change. Despite the fact he made good money touring, Eddie

Cunningham's death showed Sam he needed to work smarter, not harder. He was still in the midst of Keen and Specialty Records' bitter struggle for his publishing rights. He felt powerless because he had no voice in the matter and vowed never to be put in that situation again.

As Sam recovered from his car accident, he used the idle time to review his career status. Songs like his August 1958 release of "Win Your Love for Me" did well (peaking at #4 R&B, #22 pop), but where that was once a blessing, it was now a concern. He started focusing on the limited opportunities a small label like Keen presented and knew he needed to find a bigger distribution outlet. Once he found that outlet, he knew that things would have to be different in order to avoid another Specialty/Keen fiasco. During his accident recovery period, Sam began to see reality with profound clarity—he needed to seize greater control over his career and there was no better time than the present to start. It's funny how a little near-death experience can be such an effective motivating factor.

Just as S.R. Crain mentored Sam during his period with the Soul Stirrers, Sam now looked to pattern his efforts after the ex-Pilgrim Traveler J.W. Alexander. All three men were Gospel veterans and Sam remained close to the Pilgrim group members even after they had made the gospel-to-pop conversion to The Travelers. Sam knew that J.W. had an enterprising nature, and even though his music publishing company was little more than an idea at this point, he had at least had the where-withal to get the ball rolling. At Sam's request, the men decided to partner up and Sam Cooke and S.R Crain became co-owners of KAGS Music Corporation. The same threesome would also go on to form an ASCAP publishing company, Malloy Music Corporation, and SAR Records, Inc., so named for the founders Sam, Alexander and Roy.

SAR Records, historic in the fact that no black recording artist had ever formed a record label, would become Sam's creative outlet. Deep in his heart he still loved gospel and the first act he courted to the label was his ex-group, The Soul Stirrers. Sam convinced the Stirrers to reject an offer from Vee-Jay Records and join SAR instead—if for no other reason than to utilize his songwriting talents. The offer was one the Stirrers couldn't refuse and in September of 1959, they released "Wade in the Water," written by Sam Cooke and J.W. Alexander. In a two and a half year period, Sam had gone from cashing checks as a Soul Stirrer to signing the group's checks as the man in charge.

As word got around Sam was looking for a record deal with a major company, he attracted the attention of several labels, but narrowed his choices down to two—RCA and Atlantic Records. Sam weighed the pros and cons of both offers, but when he demanded his deal include the ownership of his publishing rights, Atlantic immediately balked. Sam had learned from his mistakes, first by letting Art Rupe's Venice Music control the publishing rights of his gospel works and his early pop demos, then by not signing a formal agreement with Keen before "You Send Me" took off. The latter oversight caused a rift between him and Bumps Blackwell that would never be mended professionally. Sam learned the hard way that publishing rights were *the* valued asset in the music industry. He learned that when artists covered his songs (several had tried their hand at "You Send Me," for example), it was the owner of the publishing rights, not the artist, which benefited. Publishing rights represented an artist's main avenue of royalties for both today and tomorrow, and their sacrifice is not unlike a mother putting her newborn baby up for adoption. If that analogy holds true, then the poet William Ross Wallace was right: The hand that rocks the cradle *is* the hand that rules the world.

Sam signed a deal with RCA in January of 1960 that not only guaranteed his financial security through the ownership of his publishing rights, it provided him a $100,000 signing bonus as well. Sam Cooke had quietly and discreetly tilted the power scale more towards the artist, and in one pen stroke inked a deal that would impact music history from that day forward.

Chapter Seven

Finding His Way at RCA

SAM STRUGGLED IN HIS EARLY days at RCA. Paired with the production team of Hugo Peretti and Luigi Creatore, his first single on the label was a syrupy love ballad aimed at the crossover market that failed miserably in its sincerity. Despite heavy promotion, "Teenage Sonata" didn't move the black audience and it didn't impress the white audience, peaking at #22 R&B and only #50 on the pop charts. Sam's second single, "You Understand Me," fared even worse. To add insult to injury, he released the uninspired album "Cooke's Tour" in which Sam sings about cities around the world. Not used to sub-standard releases, Sam had to wonder had his decision to sign the big contract blown up in his face.

Sam went to RCA with the sole intention of becoming a crossover success. He figured that if any company knew how to market and develop his talent, it would be a company with the size and history of RCA; he was already aware of how they had made Harry Belafonte a household name. RCA, in turn, bought into the idea as well, believing Sam's charm and good looks were a marketable commodity. They felt that if any black artist could successfully penetrate the young white market, it would be someone as dashing and polished as Sam Cooke. Yet they (i.e. Sam and RCA together) struggled to find the proper formula coming out of the gate.

I liked most of the songs he recorded during the Specialty/Keen years (1957-59), and I asked myself what was different once he made the switch to RCA. One of the problems had to do with the songs themselves. Just as "Lovable" had failed as his pop debut, songs like "Teenage Sonata" and "You Understand Me" were suffering the same fate for the same reason: weak material. Sam, as talented and as gifted a singer he was, seemed to perform best when armed with quality material. Sure, he could go through the motions; the beauty of his voice alone was enough to captivate the listener. But his true fans could detect when Sam plodded mechanically through a song, and as a result, these songs didn't sell very well.

There was also the problem of freedom. While at Keen, no one in management seemed to know how to create and promote a hit record. In fact, the owners didn't even really have much of a label until Sam Cooke came along. Consequently, the owners cleared the kitchen and let Sam whip up the meal. Not only was Sam the Head Chef, he had written a lot of the recipes in the Cooke-book as well. When the meal was done, he'd hit the road and pass out samples until everybody stormed the kitchen begging for more. Keen's only role was to make sure they provided enough "plates" for second helpings.

RCA, Sam saw, handled things a bit differently. They were more methodical, more calculating. RCA had a regimen in mind that had worked before, and they felt that there was no reason to reinvent the wheel. This particular crossover project did present some challenges, but RCA had been in the business of developing, marketing, and promoting singers for years. After all, Sam Cooke was just another singer, wasn't he?

While Sam and the RCA execs were planning their next course of attack in New York, the owners of Keen Records were busy scouring their Los Angeles vaults for marketable Sam Cooke demos among the tapes they still owned. They came across "Wonderful World" and released the song in April of 1960. Sam had written the song himself and it was cut from the same cloth as the previous million-seller songs he had written, "You Send Me" and "I'll Come Running Back to You." When Sam wrote, he wrote to appeal to the common man about common life occurrences, and he seemed to be at his best when he didn't over-sing a song. Hence, the heart-felt "Wonderful World," about a love-struck young man who seemed to know more about the simplicity of love than the complexity of his schoolwork (note the irony here), was commercially more successful than the angst-ridden "Teenage Sonata." "Wonderful World" eventually went to #12 on the pop charts and #2 on the R&B charts and became Sam's third million-selling single.

RCA executives, not budging on the belief they knew what was best for Sam, tried to force more cookie-cutter material onto the market. Besides the singles, they'd released another second-rate album called "Hits of the Fifties," which featured Sam singing the Nat King Cole classic "Mona Lisa." It was a great crossover hit for Nat, why wouldn't it work for Sam? The truth of the matter was that Nat King Cole and Sam Cooke, though both black, were distinctively different individuals. The mistake RCA had made, once again, was trying to fit a multi-faceted peg into an ultra-square hole.

It wasn't until they released "Chain Gang" in July of 1960 did they break through with a million-selling single of their own. Truth be told, it was with reservations RCA released the song, afraid the white audience would reject the sensitive subject matter. After all, chain gangs were mostly perceived as being made up of black inmates, a fact lending to why this was such a quirky idea from the start.

"Chain Gang" had been one of the first songs Sam recorded when he signed with RCA in early January. However, in the documentary "Sam Cooke: Legend," producer Luigi Creatore had the audacity to try and suggest that they released the song after successfully solving the Sam Cooke enigma. What they did, in fact, was muddle through classics and remakes as they watched Keen's Cooke-written "Wonderful World" soar up the charts without them.

Creatore also stated they wanted to keep Sam "what he was" when in fact they were doing exactly the opposite. How else would you explain a kid from Bronzeville singing on "Cooke's Tour" about places he had never been, like the Irish port of Galway Bay? Its one thing to admit RCA had been experimenting with effective marketing strategies for the crossover, and that they released "Chain Gang" when nothing else seemed to work. That I can understand. If all along Hugo & Luigi felt "Chain Gang" was a hit record but RCA executives were reluctant to release the song, I can understand that as well. But please, Luigi, don't tell me you were trying to keep him "what he was." "Wonderful World" had to chart before you realized it was probably best to let Sam Cooke be Sam Cooke.

The blame didn't fall solely on Hugo & Luigi and RCA. Sam was the one actually giving the OK to these projects. If anything, *Sam* was just as guilty of reinventing the wheel. His success at Keen came from singing quality songs he felt comfortable with, and he'd find out that once he took the same approach at RCA, his singles would be at the top of the charts on a regular basis. I once addressed this issue in an interview with David and Charles:

"When Sam was with Keen, some of the material he wrote, other songs were remakes, but on the whole he was pretty successful. When he signed with RCA, it seemed like they kept sending him down the wrong paths until they decided to let him do his own thing."

"Do you know what that was?" David answered. "It wasn't so much that it was RCA's doing; it was Sam trying to figure out how to get across to the white audience."

"When we were up in Canada, Sam even tried (singing in) a Top Hat and Tails," Charles added.

"So he was just feeling it out then?"

"Yeah!" both uncles answered at the same time.

"Then as he got comfortable with himself, after so many hits, he said 'I don't need to do this anymore,'" David continued. "That's why I've said he was such a success going back to the Copa. The first time he did songs out of his realm. It wasn't that anybody was telling him what to do; he was just trying to conform. Then when he failed he said 'I've got to go another way.' Nobody was telling him which direction to take; this was just something he had to experience."

Granted, not all of Sam's works could be Top 40 hits. The early RCA releases, probably his most unnatural and unsuccessful works, were, at one time, somewhat painful for me to listen to. Songs like "If You Were the Only Girl," "Jeanie with the Light Brown Hair" and even my mom's favorite, "I Belong to Your Heart," to me made Sam sound like a fish out of water. Don't get me wrong, Sam sings these songs beautifully, but after listening to them my immediate reaction is—well, nothing. The general public had the same sentiment because these songs were not commercial successes. Unfortunately, it's not just these songs. The misguided "Cooke's Tour" album has always left me unsatisfied, the big band sound of songs like "Don't Get Around Much Anymore" and "Exactly Like You" off of the "My Kind of Blues" LP sound dated even for his times, and tongue-in-cheek singles like the Keen B-side "Ee Yi Ee Yi Oh" are just downright corny. These were all songs Sam covered, and I used to wonder why he even bothered recording them in the first place, but when I take into account that Sam was trying to find the formula to crossover success, I have to respect the fact that he went through an experimental phase before he finally settled into his own.

RCA undoubtedly felt they dodged a bullet with "Chain Gang's" acceptance. But once the reality of back-to-back million-selling singles began to sink in, RCA realized they were on to something big. They saw that as a songwriter Sam possessed an acute social awareness that made him capable of reaching the masses like few artists could, and quickly looked to Sam for more of his material. The next three singles they'd release—"Sad Mood," "That's It—I Quit—I'm Moving On," and "Cupid"— were all Top 40 Pop hits, with "That's It" being the only one not written by Sam (and charting the lowest out of the three). "Cupid," released in May of 1961, peaked at #17 Pop and #20 R&B and is one of Sam's most popular songs to this day. Once the RCA brass cleared their chefs out of the kitchen, they discovered Sam's soup tasted that much better.

One of the factors that made Sam Cooke a legendary artist was his amazing versatility. While Sam is often identified as the premier Soul artist, there are instances in which he sings quality non-Soul material that is simply fantastic. The 1961 "Swing Low" LP is a shining example of this. Sam, for a change, was not singing around a theme—hits of the fifties, cities of the globe, blues standards, etc.—this was the first RCA album that actually had a touch of Sam's flavor. The LP included an "acceptable" gospel song in the old Negro spiritual "Swing Low, Sweet Chariot," as well as the Sam Cooke compositions "You Belong to Me" and "If I Had You." Sam even did justice to the folk classic "Grandfather's Clock." On top of that, his renditions of "They Call the Wind Maria" and "I'm Just a Country Boy," while not indicative of the musical direction he'd eventually take, are top-notch none the less.

Sam's string of five hit singles (four on RCA, one on Keen) made a statement to RCA that he had an idea of what the public wanted to hear, and as a result Sam sought greater artistic control. He wanted to break away from writing to please the teen white crowd and focus on more adult-oriented music that both white and black audiences could appreciate. "Chain Gang" proved Sam could achieve Pop success even from a controversial subject and "Cupid" proved he could write songs that were equally accepted across both markets. He no longer needed to aim for the teenaged crowd as he had done in his earlier years. After all, by the end of 1961 Sam was almost 31 and two years into a marriage to Linda's mother, Barbara Campbell. He had fathered their second daughter Tracey and his son, Vincent, had been born that November. The teen market aside, Sam had started to figure out what constituted a hit record, and with each of the past five singles he tightened his grip on the pulse of mainstream America. He sought and received greater input as a producer and this, in turn, minimized the roles of Hugo Peretti and Luigi Creatore. Sam still recognized them as being in charge of his production, but he felt he wanted to reach crowds they knew little about—his true black core fan base.

If RCA was Sam's boardroom, then SAR represented his playground. Gospel was still his true love, but Sam knew the financial opportunities in the budding R&B market were too great to ignore. He was constantly recruiting new acts to SAR and by September of 1961, the label had its first hit record with the Sims Twins' version of "Soothe Me." "Soothe Me" was a variation of a song Sam originally wrote with LeRoy Crume for the Soul Stirrers, "Lead Me Jesus," but like he had done with "Lovable" four years earlier, Sam took advantage of the inherent soulfulness gospel music possessed. He felt the song's chorus, "lead me Jesus, lead me," would be more successful in its pop translation "soothe me baby, soothe me" and he was right. Sam, in effect, took "Lead Me Jesus" out of the church and into the streets, and while some gospel patrons frowned on moves like this, pop patrons boosted the song to #4 on the R&B charts and #42 on the Pop charts.

Sam now signed new acts on SAR with the pop charts in mind. Gospel music was once the backbone of the black community, but he was aware its commercial appeal had been surpassed exponentially by secular forms of music, most notably R&B and Rock & Roll. Sam, always one to spot a trend, launched the label just as black music was gaining mainstream popularity, and it wasn't long before ex-gospel singers saw the opportunities as well. Ex-Highway QC and Soul Stirrer Johnnie Taylor, and former Pilgrim Traveler lead singer Kylo Turner were now pop artists on SAR. The teenaged Womack Brothers, who Sam originally met as small children singing in a Cleveland church, would record a gospel single in 1961, but by 1962 make the transformation to The Valentinos. "Looking for a Love" (a rework of "Couldn't Hear Nobody Pray") was their first pop single and the song peaked at #8 R&B, #72 Pop.

One way in which Sam exercised his greater artistic freedom at RCA was by hand-picking his supporting cast. His reunion with Rene Hall, the orchestral arranger of "You Send Me" while at Specialty and "I'll Come Running Back to You" after he left the label, would be monumental in taking Sam to the next plateau in 1962. Sam shared a musical connection with Hall that he didn't have with Hugo & Luigi and when it came to achieving a particular sound, the two were in sync from the first note to the last. If Sam were Michael Jordan, then Rene Hall would be Scottie Pippen; the two fed off of one another in a way that could only be described as magical. The only drawback was that the arranger Hall and his musicians worked out of L.A. and Sam had to convince his bosses to let him record outside of their watchful New York eye. RCA was none too pleased by this arrangement (no pun intended), but caved in to the demands of one of their biggest stars.

Sam Cooke's independence was starting to annoy the head honchos at RCA. He was supposed to be another artist in their stable, a disposable asset once the spotlight faded. But the tiger cub they once thought was so cute and cuddly had now started to grow teeth. What were once requests were now closer to demands as Sam got more and more comfortable with the fact that the label needed him as much as he needed them. Both parties were aware he was becoming a hit-making machine, and when there was an issue of relative importance to him, he'd flex his star power muscle to eventually get things to go his way. "Sometimes he'd talk to them like dogs," Charles would say. With his unprecedented publishing deal, Sam was raking in the big bucks from both the parent company and his SAR Records/KAGS Music ventures. This tiger cub no longer meowed; he was now beginning to roar.

A perfect example of the type of power move Sam was capable of occurred in a late-1961 business transaction. According to Joe McEwen, Sam and J.W. Alexander won a lawsuit for ownership of their Keen masters, which included material recorded while at the label as well as "You Send Me," brought over from Specialty. The two business partners wanted to sell the masters to an uninterested RCA, so what they did was fake the release of a Cooke-written song from the masters, "Just for You," on the duo's SAR label. RCA, furious at the idea of having to compete in the market against their own artist, had no choice but to buy the masters from KAGS. In the long run, RCA would make millions off of the $15,000 they paid for the Keen masters, proving that at the time neither side saw their potential value. But in the short term RCA was smarting from the embarrassment of being outfoxed by Sam Cooke and J.W. Alexander.

The one constant that made the relationship palatable, however, was the fact that Sam kept churning out hits. Rock and Roll was no longer seen as a passing fad. The recording industry was showing historic profits and artists like Sam Cooke meant big business. If RCA wasn't already satisfied with Sam's achievements, then Sam's collaboration with Rene Hall from late 1961 to his death in '64 would propel him to a star of stratospheric proportions.

Their initial order of business would be to address Rock and Roll's first dance craze, the Twist. The original version of "The Twist" was written and released as a B-side by Hank Ballard and the Midnighters in late 1958. The song was written in response to a dance in which couples hugged and simultaneously twisted their hips to the song's rhythm. The relative closeness and suggestive hip movements were perceived by adults as being too risqué for the times. Still the song was popular enough with teenagers to earn Ballard a booking on "American Bandstand," a booking which he and his group failed to attend.

An unknown named Chubby Checker covered the song in mid-1959. Checker spent the next year promoting the song and dance and earned an August 1960 booking on "American Bandstand" which he dutifully honored. His sanitized version was the first to demonstrate the dance with couples separated, sending the song to the #1 Pop spot in late 1960 where it stayed on the charts for sixteen weeks into 1961.

What happened next got Sam's attention: Checker's "Twist" re-entered the pop charts in late 1961 as adults now caught on, and by January of 1962 was back at #1 again, the only time in music history this phenomenon's occurred. Sam, constantly watching music trends, went to work on his *own* single in late 1961. He released "Twistin' the Night Away" in January of 1962, coinciding with "The Twist" hitting its second #1 stride. Sam's song would ride "The Twist's" wave all the way to #9 Pop and #1 R&B, giving him his fifth million-selling single in five years, and his third under the orchestration of Rene Hall. Sam's ever-sharp awareness had paid off once again.

Sam was in a zone and struck while the iron was hot. That February, he'd release an album called "Twistin' the Night Away" to further milk the twisting fad. The album, recorded in RCA's Hollywood studio, was clearly under Sam's production. Besides the title song, Sam threw the listener every conceivable twist combination; he twisted in the old town tonight on one song, he twisted in the kitchen with Dinah on another, and did the "Camptown Twist" on still a third. He even did a cover of the Ballard/Checker "Twist" that started it all. The album also contained a few Sam originals, most notably the bluesy "Somebody Have Mercy." "Mercy" would be released as a B-side single later in the year and reach #3 on the R&B charts in its own right. Sam was hitting both the pop and R&B markets head-on. The twisting spoofs, clearly not his most creative works, were specifically designed to capitalize on the raging dance phenomenon. The other songs were in-your-face, take-it-or-leave-it Sam Cooke.

Never one to rest on his laurels, Sam went to work on the soulful single, "Bring It On Home to Me" which he released in May of 1962. To me, this song and "Twistin' the Night Away" are two Sam Cooke classics which have best withstood the test of time. I can play either song over and over again and feel the same satisfaction from the first time to the last. The same could be said for most of the songs he released in the Hall era, including "Somebody Have Mercy." This period produced Sam Cooke's finest work as a pop artist.

"Bring It On Home to Me" was a smash hit (#13 pop, # 2 R&B) because of the variety of musical forms that seem to capture you from the opening note and not let go. The piano and snare drum intro has blues written all over it, and the catchy melody makes your head bob from the initial downbeat. Sam and Lou Rawls hit the first verse with that good ole gospel fervor. By the time the chorus kicks in, the two veterans fall back on a call-and-response pleading whose origin dates back to field workers during slavery times. If you can listen to this song and not move *something*, check your pulse, you may have to cancel the holidays. This song is pure Soul, and it grabs you from the very start. All you have to do is sit back, close your eyes and let Sam and Lou bring it on home from there.

Lou Rawls with Soul Stirrer
R.B. Robinson, Los Angeles, 1952
(Photo courtesy of Toni Cook
Howard)

One of the main reasons "Bring It On Home to Me" has that laid back feeling is because of Sam's choice of the ex-Pilgrim Traveler and Soul Stirrer Rawls as his response partner. The two men survived the turf wars growing up together in the tough Bronzeville neighborhood of Chicago. They extensively toured the South together as both gospel and pop artists at a time when racial tension was at its peak. They sidestepped death together in 1958 as their car slammed into the back of parked truck at well over 100 miles per hour. So to stand late night in front of a studio microphone and beg for this woman's forgiveness together almost seemed trivial. It's as if Lou is helping his old buddy out, singing to Sam's woman *with* Sam, hoping that between the two of them their call-and-response pleas would make her drop her suitcase and run back into Sam's arms. The sincerity of "Bring It On Home to Me" comes from the Sam Cooke/ Lou Rawls chemistry, and it's this chemistry that still rings true when the song is played some forty plus years later. The passion with which they deliver the song's lyrics makes it timeless, and the eclectic mix of Blues and gospel harmony in the song's music makes it Soul.

As if "Bring It On Home to Me" wasn't a big enough hit, Sam creates what can only be described as songwriting genius on the flipside. "Having a Party" was Sam's third straight Top 10 R&B single, peaking at #4 (#17 Pop). The song is a classic because of the way Sam masterfully recreates the party's atmosphere–in two short verses we know what refreshments were served, what songs were on the venue, and what dances were danced–and by the time the repetitive chorus takes us out, we actually *feel* the party's electricity! It's this catchy chorus that has the ability to uplift your entire mood and is the reason why "Having a Party" would be covered by everyone from Rod Stewart to Luther Vandross.

After a Cubs baseball game in early 2004, I was in a bar around the corner from Wrigley Field when the DJ played a cover of "Having a Party" by Southside Johnny & the Asbury Jukes. If you've ever experienced Wrigleyville after a Cubs game, win or lose you know how festive these bars can be. Some people were dancing, most were mingling, but when the DJ suddenly dropped the song's volume, the whole bar proceeded to clap their hands as they sung the chorus a cappella. He kicked the volume back up and things went back to normal, but in that brief few seconds he had managed to garner everyone's attention. Most of the patrons were in their mid 20's to upper 30's, and probably had no clue who the original artist was, but 42 years after its release, the song was still a crowd favorite.

Sam was white hot by the summer of 1962. Since RCA gave Sam the freedom to call his own shots, seven of his eight releases on the label reached the coveted Top 40, and four of those went Top 10. Only the single "Feel It," attacked by moral crusaders who questioned what "it" was, fell short. If you include Keen's release of "Wonderful World," that totaled eight Top 40, (five of those Top 10), and three million-selling singles in a two and a half year span. Even more impressive, Sam had written eight of the songs himself and was co-writer (along with Lou Adler and Herb Alpert) on the other one, "Wonderful World." To have three Top 40 singles in a calendar year was a major accomplishment for any artist. Sam had charted three Top 40 singles by the Fourth of July, and he still had more hot songs in the works.

In September he released the bluesy ballad "Nothin' Can Change This Love." In the song Sam professes his unwavering love by giving examples of the punishment he'd endure for the "apple of his eye." Paired with "Somebody Have Mercy," "Change" went to #12 Pop, #2 R&B, while the "Mercy" topped out at #70 Pop, but went #3 R&B.

Its one thing to have a string of hit records, but the way Sam was doing it was unreal. He tore up the charts with everything from Rock and Roll ("Twistin' the Night Away") to ballads ("Nothin' Can Change This Love") to R&B ("Having a Party) to blues-influenced Soul ("Bring It On Home to Me" and "Somebody Have Mercy"). The year would conclude with Sam releasing another ballad, "Send Me Some Lovin'." "Lovin'" would be the first A-side Sam hadn't written in more than 2 ½ years, but it was still a blockbuster, heading to #13 pop and #2 R&B. Sam's records were so popular across both charts, one could start to use Top *10* as his measure of success instead of the standard Top 40 used by the rest of the industry.

"Sam was so hot back then he was the buzz of the whole neighbor-hood," Agnes recalls. "Everywhere you went people were talking about 'Have you heard the new record? Have you got Sam's record?' Everybody was proud that they knew him, and proud of the fact they could tell people he was from the neighborhood. Even today they would tell you Sam never changed. That's why people were so crazy about him and his music."

Actually, not everyone was crazy about Sam because late that sum-mer a rumor started to spread that Sam was dying from leukemia. "Some people even had him dead," Agnes would add. No one knew the origin of the urban legend but it also said that he planned to leave his eyes to his friend Ray Charles. Totally unfounded, the rumor persisted for several months despite constant denials from Sam and his current manager, Jess Rand.

In October of 1962, Sam agreed to his first and only European road trip, sharing the spotlight with Little Richard around various cities in England. In some respects, this tour was a test—would Sam's laid back demeanor be overshadowed by the more flamboyant Little Richard? His records had sold well here: "Twistin' the Night Away," "Cupid" and "Chain Gang" were all Top 10 hits on England's *Billboard* equivalent, the NME Polls. It seemed that after five years he'd harnessed the likes and dislikes of the American public, but now he was in a different venue. Would his reception across the pond be the same as it was stateside?

The answer to the question would be a resounding, overwhelming "yes." While Sam and Little Richard were as different as night and day in every respect, both men's sound reflected their gospel backgrounds. With these gospel roots in mind, Sam created absolute pandemonium night after night, performing as he did in America, singing everything from 1957's "You Send Me" to the current year's "Twistin'." If ever Sam had one shred of doubt, now he was convinced: instead of giving less of himself as he had been doing in previous years, he could now add a little touch of the gospel passion he had been singing with all his life to create *his* style of music. As a result, he realized he could win over more fans doing what he did best rather than singing to appease a certain crowd.

The front and inside of a personalized Christmas card from the Cookes, 1962. The artwork is all Sam's—caricatures, calligraphy, greeting and crest. Daughter Linda signed each card by hand.

(Card courtesy of Toni Cook Howard)

Sam's work at SAR Records should not to be forgotten during this glorious run. Sam somehow managed to balance writing and producing hit after hit on RCA with signing, writing for, and producing acts on his own label. Sam seized the opportunity to sign the ex-Soul Stirrer R.H. Harris, who was now the lead singer of the Gospel Paraders. In February of 1962 Sam produced three Parader songs for the "Gospel Pearls" compilation LP that also featured the Soul Stirrers. Sam himself contributed four songs to the album: "I Thank God," "Steal Away," "Deep River," and "That's Heaven to Me." He also found time to produce the previously mentioned "Looking for a Love" by the Valentinos which peaked at #8 on the R&B charts, as well write and produce "Meet Me at the Twisting Place" (#18 R&B, #63 Pop) for his partying buddy Johnnie Morisette. Sam would later rewrite "Twisting Place" and record it as "Meet Me at Mary's Place." A testament to how times had changed, the Soul Stirrers sang background on the pop single "Mary's Place;" a gesture that had been inconceivable just a few years before.

The general arrangement between the SAR partners was that Sam would handle in-studio operations like producing, writing, and arranging, J.W. Alexander would handle legal and bookkeeping matters, and S.R. Crain would be responsible for booking the acts as well as making sure everything ran smoothly. Crain was Sam's right hand man, his eyes and ears when he was away from the office. Though their difference in age would suggest a father/son relationship, Crain was more like an older brother to Sam. But just like Sam, Crain was human; he couldn't always watch over everything, nor did he have the ability to be in more than one place at a time.

Chapter Eight

Sam Songs Say So Much

THE MARTIAL ART OF JUDO, which literally translated means "gentle way," emphasizes technique, skill, and timing, rather than the use of brute strength. One of its basic tenets is to maximize efficiency and minimize effort, to use compliance instead of resistance. If your opponent throws a punch, you're taught to fall with the flow of the punch rather than to block or resist it. The object is to not only avoid an opponent's superior strength, but to use that strength to his disadvantage.

Sam Cooke did not hold a black belt in Judo. By all accounts, he never even took a self-defense class. Nevertheless, his songwriting techniques mirrored Judo's core philosophy—he didn't try to go against the flow of his times, he simply went with it. As a result, Sam's pop songs were often mistakenly criticized as being sophomoric and simplistic. The truth is that it's his songs' simplicity which makes them timeless and invariably contributes to his status as a musical genius.

The love-struck teenager in "Wonderful World" is a perfect example of how Sam made a hit record out of a common scenario. What teenager *hasn't* gone through the distractions of love? Sam's songs were unique because he wrote them as if he were having a conversation with the listener instead of singing to the listener. This straightforward songwriting approach was such a radical departure from the norm, it was initially misunderstood. So little was thought of "You Send Me," a whisper of a song written with almost child-like innocence, it suffered the fate of being the B-side to the much more "accomplished" Gershwin classic "Summertime". "You Send Me" went on to be Sam's best selling single of all time and skyrocketed his popularity virtually overnight.

Sam was successful because he approached his craft from a sociological standpoint as much as he did a musical standpoint. When asked by Dick Clark his secret to writing hit records, Sam replied, "I think the secret is really observation. If you observe what's going on, try to figure out how people are thinking and determine the times of your day, I think you can always write something that the people will understand."

Sam's observation skills probably contributed more to his success than any other factor. Sam studied people, first of all. He studied their actions and mannerisms, the way they talked, and what they said. When he wrote a song, he used the words *they'd* use in conversation to effectively paint the picture. Let's take, for example, the 1959 single "Everybody Loves to Cha Cha Cha" which rose to #31 on the Pop charts and #2 on the R&B charts. The premise of the song is that Sam's girl doesn't know how to do the latest dance. Sam, while at the "hop," teaches her the dance, and by the end of the night she's doing it better than him.

It doesn't matter that I can't distinguish the "Cha Cha Cha" from other dances of the fifties. It doesn't matter that Sam, who couldn't dance a lick himself, had the nerve to write a song about teaching someone else the latest dance. I'm sure the question "are you kids going to the hop tonight?" would elicit a strange reaction if posed to today's teenagers. I wouldn't know Tom Dooley if he rang my doorbell, nor could I hum a few bars of "Tea for Two" if my life depended on it. The song's Latin flavor reflected a sound that was hot during that time period. Why, then, do I consider a song like this a timeless (not to be confused with dated) classic? Because as a four year old in 1970, I could recite every word as well as follow the storyline. Sam's lyrics were in the vernacular of his day, but his straightforward, conversational approach was, and still is, easy to understand.

Sam used his skills of observation to study trends and stay on top of changes in music. He made the decision to move from gospel in 1957 after watching the increased mainstream acceptance of black music. It wasn't a matter of raw talent; even at the peak of his gospel popularity, there were dozens of artists who were considered better singers than Sam Cook, including the one he replaced in the Soul Stirrers, R.H. Harris. Sam's foresight made him realize the opportunities in gospel were limited, and he made the move when he felt the time was right for a black crossover artist to make an impact.

Sam also recognized that observation was the key to an artist's longevity. How often do we see artists release the same style of music once they've had a string of successful hits? They tend to think they're giving the people what they want, when in fact over the course of time, people's desires change (Sam's posthumous dance hits "Shake" and "Yeah, Man" were examples of a new Soul sound he had in mind). These artists can have all the talent in the world, but without the flexibility to change with the times, they invariably wind up on the "Where Are They Now?" segment of entertainment news shows.

Sam didn't have that problem. Once he was free to be himself, he focused on releasing good music both blacks and whites would buy. Sam proved he could write dance songs with a highly-charged, Rock and Roll sound like "Twistin' the Night Away" or with a slow-dance-in-the-basement, R&B flavor like "Having a Party". "Cupid" and "Wonderful World" were airy and lighthearted, and you'd be hard pressed to believe he was the same artist that wrote the grittier "Bring It On Home to Me" or the riskier "Chain Gang" had he not sung all four. The six songs I mentioned spanned a broad horizon of tastes. One thing they had in common, however, was that they all reached the top twenty on *both* the R&B and Pop charts. Sam's initial intent was to cover his bases with the whites on one side and the blacks on the other. What he hadn't anticipated was both audiences eating up everything, which of course was a good problem to have. The secret of mass appeal, Sam discovered indirectly, did not lie in giving the audience what he thought they wanted to hear, but in giving the audience good music and letting the chips fall where they may.

In 1964, Sam released the B-side single "That's Where It's At." In the song a man and a woman are enjoying each other's company to the point she begs him to stay just a little longer, bringing back memories of stolen moments and young love almost everyone can relate to. Sam's songs have a way of conjuring up certain memories in your life, memories buried so deeply they sometimes seem surreal. In this case, it may have been at the end of a high school date, when you knew you had to have your girlfriend home before her father's curfew. It may have been a forbidden love affair, one in which you had to say goodbye today in order to be able to see each other again another day. Regardless, he painted the picture of two lovers, face to face, confronting the moment in which they must part. *That's where it's at*; simple yet immensely heartfelt. I even venture to use the oxymoron "universally personal" to describe Sam's songwriting touch.

"Sam could think up a song just like that," Charles says, snapping his fingers. "All you'd have to do is give him a title if you wanted to see him do it. It was just incredible to look at Sam and see all the stuff that would go on in his head. A lot of times, if he didn't have paper, he'd take a restaurant napkin and write down what would come to him. He would write the whole song on a napkin. He'd tell Clif (guitarist Clifton White) 'Come here, Clif. Let's get together. I have a song.' They'd get together and the next thing you know, they've got a hit record. Sam was just a phenomenal dude." Charles, shaking his head, starts to get emotional. "He was *really* something else. Ain't no telling where he'd be today if he had lived."

SAR's Zelda Sands, who wrote "Looking for a Love" for The Valentinos, agreed that songwriting came to Sam with relative ease:

"Sam, J.W., and I wrote this song, "Talking Trash." We were just clowning around because people in the office used to use that lingo and I felt 'hmm, what a wonderful song title!' So Sam walks in and asks what we were doing and I told him. I said I came up with the words, but J.W. couldn't come up with the melody. He said 'let me see' and he sits down, pulls out his guitar, and that's how Sam was, he would just do it on the spot. He changed a few words, did the bridge, and that was it!"

*Sam and friends at Robert's Show Club, Chicago, 1958. From left, jazz singer
Al Hibbler (famous for the original version of "Unchained Melody"), guitarist
Clif White, Barbara Bonner Cook, S.R. Crain, friend Sam Milsap, an unidentified
neighbor, Sam, and Sam's sister Mary. Blind since birth, the signature at the bottom was
signed on Al Hibbler's behalf.*

(Photo courtesy of Toni Cook Howard)

Oddly enough, Sam got the idea for some of his songs from horsing around with the Gashouse Gang. Sam was so gifted a songwriter, he could take the simplest sound or call-and-response phrase and find use for it in a song.

"The hook from "Chain Gang," the "ooh, ahh," came from a time he had us dancing around the house when we were little kids," Gene recalls. "They had just returned from Jamaica and Sam brought back this thumb piano. Sam would play it, then sing a little verse and our response would be "ooh, ahh." That's where I think the "ooh, ahh" started." Sam used it again in "Sad Mood," released later that same year.

"The same was true for "Do You Like Good Music?" (actually titled "Yeah, Man")", Gene continued. "He would start with Gwen: 'Do you know how to Cha Cha?' and Gwen would go 'Yeah, man!', because Gwen was always a good dancer. Then he would pop out another dance: 'Well do you know how to…?' and Gwen would go 'Yeah, man!' That hook came from a night at my grandmother's house."

"It was around 1959," Charles says, remembering how the idea for "Chain Gang" came about. "We were driving through Georgia when we pulled over and watched the chain gang out there working in the fields. Then we drove about 4 or 5 miles up the road until we saw a country store. Sam said 'pull in here and get them boys some cigarettes'. We got about 5 cartons of cigarettes, divided them up and gave them to the guys. Man, they thanked us; they were so happy! Sam wrote the song that night, after we got to the hotel."

"Chain Gang" went on to sell over a million singles, peaking at #2 on both the Pop and R&B charts. Today, it's one of Sam Cooke's most identifiable records.

Sam Cooke was a perfectionist when it came to music. As an artist, he stressed the importance of clear diction, and it was probably one of the reasons his music was as universally accepted as it was. On a song like the 1958 Keen release "You Were Made for Me," for example, Sam compares how he was made for his lover to a boat made for the sea. Every time he says the word "boat" you can distinctly hear his emphasis on pronouncing the "t." The same is true for "I'll Come Running Back to You," where he clearly sounds out the words *night, bite* and *right*. Sam realized that in his day, music from black artists who sang with a noticeable slur would more than likely be categorized as "ethnic," whereas the successful crossover artist needed to appear more articulate (i.e. "less threatening") to white listeners. In the process, Sam took great pains not to alienate his black listeners, and he was successful in maintaining that delicate balance. In "Sad Mood," for example, he pronounces his words clearly and distinctly, but purposefully avoids "whitewashing" the song by leaving it in its broken-English form. As a result, the song was a Top 40 success across both markets, peaking at #29 Pop and #23 R&B.

As a producer and songwriter, Sam's musical mind worked on a level unfathomable to most, and when he had a distinctive sound he was trying to achieve, he would often have problems describing his vision to others. The veteran guitarist Clif White first thought Sam was crazy for constantly repeating "Darling, you send me" until Sam added the bridge, a little note bending on the word "you," and a few *whoa-oh's*. Then it became clear to Clif they had a marketable record. But Sam could hear the final product in his mind the whole time, then worked piece by piece to bring it together.

The same was true for the song "Chain Gang." Sam went through every instrument in RCA's studio trying to recreate the chain-rattling sound he had heard in that Georgia field. It wasn't until someone accidentally knocked a metal microphone stand against the metal legs of a stool was he satisfied he had recreated the sound in his head, and a similar "clunk" can be heard in the song today. In some cases Sam would alter instruments, putting a paper bag between guitar strings, for example, to achieve a desired sound. His level of creativity knew no bounds, and quite often his music reflected this.

With Sam's quest for perfection in mind, it's not surprising that his legendary classic "A Change Is Gonna Come" was admittedly the most difficult song he ever wrote. Inspired by Bob Dylan's "Blowin' in the Wind," he tried to transcribe Dylan's masterful use of imagery into his own common-man writing style, a task comparable to trying to squeeze toothpaste back into its tube. To simplify Dylan's sentiments, yet portray the common struggle of black people during that era with the same tenacity, Sam undoubtedly faced a nearly impossible hurdle. Sure, he could've relied on gospel techniques he'd used so successfully in the past to drain every ounce of emotion out of this song, but this effort, in his mind, had to be different. This was *his* dedication to his people's struggle. It had to be clear and concise. It had to be special. The best approach, he'd eventually discover, was to start from the outside and work his way inside. Hence, the strength of "Change" is not just in its lyrics, but in the draining tempo, the building crescendos, and an eerie horn, string, and violin accompaniment.

A little side note here: ABKCO Records holds its rights to songs in Sam's music catalog with a frightening grip. If you've ever wondered why "A Change is Gonna Come," "Shake," "Ain't that Good News" or "Good Times" aren't featured on the RCA CD set "The Man Who Invented Soul," it's because ABKCO had the power to veto their inclusion. Very recently, a network television mini-series based on the life and death of Sam Cooke was in the works but was thwarted because the network couldn't come to an agreement to use Sam's music in the film. I had initially wanted to reprint the lyrics to "A Change is Gonna Come" here, but I decided not to give ABKCO the satisfaction of denying my request. So, please, if you're familiar with the song, pretend with me we're analyzing the lyrics together.

In the opening verse, Sam paints the picture of lifelong struggle in which we envision one wandering as aimlessly as a flowing river. If we keep in mind the fact that this song was essentially a dedication to the social and political climate of the early sixties, we come to the conclusion that he was wandering aimlessly as were many other black Americans. The first line's lyrics and delivery were more than likely borrowed from 1961's "Trouble in Mind."

As with any struggle, there's a period of hopelessness, even ennui, and in the second verse, his faith even comes into question. By questioning the reality of Heaven itself, Sam surmises "We're a people stuck between the harshness of everyday life and an unseen, unknown afterlife." Here we've hit what is one of the song's darkest moments. But since it's always darkest before the dawn—as the chorus and song's title keeps reminding us—we're down but not out.

The third verse fast forwards us to modern day America, 1964. Blacks at that time were forced to use separate washrooms, hotels, and water fountains and had "colored" sections reserved for them in most diners. According to Sam, the social climate is so tense even his usual hangouts aren't safe anymore. The verse was deleted on the single, possibly for fear of sounding too radical, but appears on the album *Ain't That Good News*.

In the refrain, it seems as if he discovers he has hit rock bottom. His "brother" has not only refused to help him, but adds insult to injury by ridiculing his efforts. It's been suggested that the "brother" he's knocked down by is white oppression, but I disagree, in fact I feel it's just the opposite. By giving the impression he's going "home," I feel he literally means the black community, where he finds fragmentation and a lack of unity. This verse is symbolic of the inevitable confrontation of the younger, more militant generation seeking advice from an older, more passive generation, and being scolded for trying to change what "has been" all their lives. Prayer seems to be his last option and his prayers are answered in the form of the civil rights movement itself. In the closing stanza, he portrays a renewed faith, a light at the end of the tunnel, if you will—where he thought he'd reached the end of his rope, he now finds strength to "carry on."

In order to create the desired mood of the song, emphasis was shifted to the aura of the music in the background. The result is a musical sound so powerful that its intensity was never rivaled in any other of Sam's recordings. The success of this song lies in the fact that he laced carefully chosen lyrics with subtle metaphors and a haunting musical background. From the lingering strings, to the crashing cymbals, to the weariness with which Sam delivers the lyrics, The Man Who Invented Soul seems to have poured his soul into every note of this song.

Personally, I've always been fascinated by the contrast between the naive innocence of "You Send Me" as Sam's first crossover hit and the intense political consciousness of "A Change is Gonna Come" as his swan song. When considered the book-ends to his pop career, the two songs mirror his progression in life itself—as Sam matured and his social awareness became more complex, so did the adult theme and lyrical content of his music.

"A Change is Gonna Come," covered by everyone from the Charlie Daniels Band to the Jackson 5, is arguably the cornerstone of Sam Cooke's legacy. Unlike the chart-topping "You Send Me," however, the song only went to #9 on the R&B charts and no higher than #31 on the Pop charts. The rationale behind this is probably why I don't listen to it as often as I do his other works, even though I love the song and what it stands for: it's a song that's so dark it has to be taken in doses; it stirs so much emotion within, you almost have to be in the mood to listen to it. If you've ever made your own compilation of Sam Cooke favorites, chances are you put that song towards the end rather than the beginning.

I believe that with Sam's unexpected death and the mysterious circumstances which surrounded the case, the listening public wasn't always "in the mood." Sam had created an enigma; a song so moving, it couldn't be endured long enough to get the spins of a normal pop record. He wanted a song to complement Dylan's "Blowin' in the Wind," (notice I didn't say rival) and in the end he had achieved just that.

"Sam said that song scared him," David and Charles both stated in separate interviews, and in retrospect one can see why. I've never experienced the impact of living in a Jim Crow society, yet I can feel his desperation in the song. "Change" was a song of pain, then loss of faith (*that* admission from a man raised in church is scary in itself), and then, in the refrain, the realization your own "brother" fails you in your hour of need.

In the last verse however, a blinding yellow sun breaks over the horizon as the dark clouds of past tribulation part. It's as if Sam, in the song, has immediately found his second wind. Having lived the harrowed past, what gives him such sudden hope for the unforeseen future?

If you take a look at American society during that period, times seemed to have been changing as rapidly as the bleak mood of the refrain changed into the hopeful fourth verse. If "Change" represented a chronological history of blacks in America since slavery, the period from hopelessness to feeling he has enough strength to endure represented the turbulent changes of the 50's and early 60's.

By 1964, Rosa Parks had brought national attention to the second-class treatment of blacks in Birmingham. *Brown vs. Board of Education's* precedence for school desegregation had been in place for ten years. Martin Luther King had described his "dream" on the steps of the Lincoln Memorial before a crowd of over 100,000, and had declared "1963 is not an end, but a beginning." Malcolm X and Muhammad Ali were constantly giving new rise to the militant black voice. Young black teens and college students were defying the passiveness of earlier generations by staging demonstrative marches, sit-ins, and protests all throughout the South. With the rising sun came newly-sprouted buds of hope which patterned the previously barren horizon. They manifested themselves in the form of hundreds of striking garbage workers in Memphis, donning black and white picket signs that read "I Am A Man." The era of Civil Rights was an indication that a new day was dawning and that yes indeed, a change was gonna come.

Simplistic? Maybe. Effortless? It seemed so. Timeless? In some cases, yes. Whatever you believe about Cooke-written songs, the truth is he had an uncanny knack of capturing a feeling and turning it into a hit. Songwriters such as Curtis Mayfield wrote with greater depth and intensity, but never came close to the commercial success and crossover acceptance of Sam Cooke. And while Sam never reached the status of Presley or Sinatra, how much of their material did they write? Sam could write for the common man about common issues with the simplicity of "Only Sixteen," "Cupid" or "Wonderful World," then summarize the struggles of an oppressed culture with songs as socially complex as "Chain Gang" or "A Change is Gonna Come." At either end of the spectrum, Sam possessed an immense talent that often baffled veteran musicians and music critics alike.

I recently attended a fundraiser thrown by a group of "silver foxes," and I watched their dance habits as certain oldies were played. Some of the songs, like Al Green's "I'm Still in Love with You," and many of the Motown and Marvin Gaye hits got a warm if not enthusiastic response. But when the DJ played "Twistin' the Night Away," the place went absolutely nuts! Young and old crowded the dance floor and danced so frantically, the DJ had to play it twice in a row and even again at the end of the party. Several people at the party commented on how they saw me singing along and couldn't believe I knew the lyrics. I wanted to tell them my theory about good music being eternal and having the ability to transcend all age barriers, but at the time we were having a party, and I just didn't think they would care very much.

Chapter Nine

Live at the Harlem Square Club

SAM ENDED 1962 ON TOP of his professional career, but the same couldn't be said of his personal life. Sam loved the "concept" of family, and he loved Barbara and their children Linda, Tracey and Vincent individually, but he wasn't exactly the ideal father figure. Recording in Los Angeles should've meant more time at home, but Sam often spent his evenings rubbing shoulders amongst L.A.'s night life. In addition, his years on the road and his immense popularity helped to retard rather than reinforce a monogamous mindset. There were various affairs with not only major recording artists, but with silver screen starlets as well. (These women, household names in the '60's and afterward, shall remain nameless here.) Sam found that with swarms of beautiful women at his disposal, finding one to adorn his arm wasn't all that difficult.

At one time, Barbara had been that woman adorning Sam's arm. They were known around town as the kind of couple that closed many a night-club in their day, most notably their main hotspot, the California Club. They may not have been the perfect pair for each other, but they shared a long history. They dated as teenagers, had a child together in their early twenties, and were there for each other through the transition from humble beginnings to a comfort level most people only dream about. As the years progressed, however, various factors made Sam withdraw more and more from Barbara. For starters, Sam didn't approve of Barbara's "social habits," and they were a constant topic of argument. Barbara in the meantime was dealing with her own dilemma; she was hurt by the number of women Sam had on the side, but also enjoyed the fancy home, cars and clothes of her Hollywood lifestyle.

Sam and Barbara Campbell line up for the wedding photographer, October 1959. The ceremony took place at Barbara's grandmother's house.

Papa Cook is all smiles as Sam kisses his bride. Standing to the left is Sam's best man, S.R. Crain. To the right is the matron of honor, Barbara's twin sister, Beverly.

Sam relaxes with friends after the ceremony.

(Photos courtesy of Toni Cook Howard)

Sam's wedding reception, held at Rev. Cook's Chicago home. The men in the photograph, l to r, are Sam's brother Charles, "Duck" Hoskins, Sam, and childhood friend Sonny Benson. The young girl receiving the cup is Sam's niece, Gwen. The other two ladies are unidentified.

(*Photo courtesy of Gwendolyn Greene*)

Despite their history together, there was a restlessness within their relationship which never seemed to go away. It may have stemmed from the fact that Sam knew Barbara was never the true love of his life. That title belonged to Dorothy "Dot" Holloway, a wholesome young beauty from Washington, D.C. Sam had met at a Soul Stirrers concert years before. Blessed with a model's face and an hour-glass figure, she was the only woman known to have turned Sam to putty. "Sam *gushed* whenever he was around her," is how my mother described it. Sam had many meaningless sexual conquests, but the romance he shared with Dot was the kind reminiscent of old Hollywood movies. He placed her on a pedestal above no other, and though their lives would take separate paths over the years, they would always find ways to be together. Sam and Dot had the type of relationship that whenever they'd reunite, it was as if they had never been apart at all:

"I was seventeen and Sam had just started off with the Stirrers when we first met (in Washington, D.C., 1951). He saw me and my mother at a show and wanted to know who I was. He asked my mother if it were OK if we went and got a sandwich after the program. I told him 'you need to ask *me*, not my mother!' But it started from that."

"Every time he'd come to town, my mother would fix dinner for him. He loved her sweet potato pie. He talked to his parents about me and they started writing me letters, until he finally took me (to Chicago) to meet them...After a while he would send for me to meet him in different places. No matter where we were or what we would do, I would always stand back because the women always wanted to be around him. And he used to say to me 'why you don't never come up and get me? I need to be rescued from these people!' I said 'but these are your people; these are your fans' and he would say 'yeah, but I want to be near *you*.' I would stand back a lot, but he would always come and get me. He would always find me through the crowd and come and get me. He was just a gentle, sweet, loving person."

"We had a lot of fun. It was a happy, happy time in my life." Her voice trailed off as she reflected romantic memories. "He would paint for me. That was his hobby–painting. He would paint beautiful pictures for me in his spare time. He would draw me all the time. I had one picture of me–pencil-drawn—that he did in New York, but I can't find it now. We did a lot of things together, went a lot of places. Then he asked me about marriage. He moved me to Chicago and gave me a ring which I still have. But when Dee-Dee told him she was pregnant (falsely, from California), I called the whole thing off. At the time I couldn't understand why he would be bothered with anyone else but me! I left Chicago, but we really didn't break it off because we always did meet back up and see each other. He never stopped calling, never stopped seeing me. From the first day we met, we've always been together. We've never, ever stopped being together."

Dorothy "Dot" Holloway when Sam met her at age 17, 1951.

(Photo courtesy of Dorothy Holloway Coates)

Besides Sam's romance with Dot Holloway, certain events contributed to Sam's emotional detachment form Barbara. SAR's former Office Manager and Cooke family friend Zelda Sands remembers that back in 1962 when Tracey was about two years old, she almost drowned in the family pool. According to Zelda, Tracey had been in a little pool chair that had somehow managed to tilt over. Zelda swam over and rescued her, but Tracey had been under water for about thirty seconds. "When they're that young, their little lungs fill up so quickly," she added. "But I'm the one who saved Tracey."

It was too early to realize this incident would set an eerie precedent, but Sam's change in attitude reflected his disgust in Barbara. He poured himself into his work, logging heavy hours at RCA's Hollywood recording studio, SAR's offices, or in the guest house he'd converted into an at-home studio. More and more Sam left Barbara at home and would go out alone, sometimes partying all night. Either out of loneliness or spite, Barbara would find ways to occupy her time, and as a result add fuel to an already dysfunctional marriage. Zelda remembered one rather awkward evening at the Cooke residence in which after dinner Barbara stood up before Sam and the kids and announced "OK, I have a date, now," and put on her coat and left. "I'm sitting there at the table, left with her family," Zelda recalls. "It felt very peculiar."

No matter how hot or cold his relationship with Barbara ran, Sam adored his children and tried to include them in his life as much as possible. By the time Linda was nine, he had appointed her his "personal secretary." Whenever he was on the road, Linda always knew his daily itinerary down to the hour, and this inclusion allowed him to keep in constant contact with his oldest daughter. She would document his tour schedule and always had his contact numbers. If something changed in his schedule, she'd be the first to know about it. Likewise, if he had any messages back home, Linda would note the name and contact number of the person that called. It was a job Linda took very seriously and performed rather well.

Unfortunately, his relationship with the children he had before his marriage to Barbara was never as close (there had been two more: Sharon (Moore) Cooke in New Orleans and Keith Bolling in Philadelphia, both born in 1957). Sam visited his children and sent the mothers money on a regular basis, but with seven children around the country, it was impossible for him to be there for all of them in the traditional sense.

Sam realized he'd woven a pretty tangled paternity web over the years, and he tried to make the situation work as best he could. Sam's five-year marriage to Dee-Dee had ended in 1958. Less than a year after the divorce, she was the fatal victim of an automobile accident. In 1959 Sam once again wanted to marry Dot Holloway, but he felt guilty about the several "mini-families" he had around the country already, so he focused on settling down with one of his children's mothers. Paula's mother Evelyn Jackson had since gotten married, and he no longer had romantic involvement with Connie Bolling in Philadelphia, Marine Somerville in Cleveland, or Laverne Moore (Sharon's mother) in New Orleans. In the end, however, Sam was concerned about Barbara Campbell's involvement with a street hustler named Fred "Diddy" Dennis and his exposure to their daughter, so he ended up marrying her. At the time, Dot understood and respected Sam's decision. "He already had Linda, and he was trying to make things right," she would say.

To compensate for a less than perfect home life, Sam immersed himself in his music. He began 1963 with one of the most historic tour dates in his career. While his appearance at Miami's Harlem Square Club was just one of many shows in which Sam brought the house to its knees, it marked the only time one of his all-black, "Chitlin' Circuit" concerts would be recorded with the intent of being distributed as a live album. The Harlem Square Club was in the heart of Miami's 'hood, and the clientele there didn't want to hear any teenage sonatas. They wanted grit, sweat, and soul and they packed the club some two thousand strong to hear the man they knew could bring it—Sam Cooke.

Most of America identified Sam Cooke with light-hearted Pop songs. More recently they'd heard flashes of R&B and Soul in songs like "Having a Party" and "Bring It On Home to Me," but a lot of his true passion was lost due to his quest for popular appeal. One criticism commonly echoed from black and white listeners alike is that Sam's Pop music tends to be more diluted–less "soulful," if you will–than other artists in his genre. While its true legends like Jackie Wilson, Ray Charles and James Brown carried a certain amount of "blackness" in their music, it should be noted that Sam Cooke *intentionally* sought to conquer the crossover market a lot of black artists either stumbled upon or were typecast into. Too often Sam's Pop career is hastily dismissed as not being "black" enough when instead it should be recognized for what it truly was–a calculated attempt to reach as large an audience as possible by utilizing his cross-cultural appeal.

Once Sam stepped away from the spotlight of mainstream America, however, there was a sizable element that saw Sam's true passion come through in his live shows. Be it gospel or pop, the Sam Cooke they knew would reach back and give the crowd a teeth-rattling, bone-shaking performance as he grinded his voice until they reached a climactic elation. One of the main reasons Sam had such a strong black following was because he could adjust his focus from spiritual rapture to sexual rapture, and his intertwining style was capable of capturing both audiences. At a live pop concert, Sam often reverted to his church roots. "Sam sang like Papa preached," Agnes would often say. At a live gospel show, Sam built an intensity that would resonate throughout the whole church. His gospel fans never forgot this intensity, and despite Sam's biggest fears, he never lost his popularity among them. As a matter of fact, less than two weeks before his date at the Harlem Square Club, Sam brought down the house as a special guest on a Soul Stirrers New Year's Eve program. Sam never lost his love for Gospel, and the adulation of the New Year's Eve crowd proved that Gospel still loved Sam as well.

But now Sam stood before his "other" audience on a Saturday night in a rough section of Miami. Never fazed, the concert stage is where he was a master at his craft. Whether gospel or pop, Sam had a way of sensing what it would take to set an audience off, and once he found that nerve, he worked it and worked it and worked it until you were physically and emotionally unable to take any more.

"Sam would just kill them!" Charles recalls. "He had them shouting in the aisles, dancing, and fainting all over. But this was an every night thing, Harlem Square was no different. He would just kill them every place he'd go!"

Sam started off the Harlem Square program with "Feel It." This may have seemed like an odd choice seeing that this was Sam's only song in the past few years that hadn't charted due to concerns about its vulgarity. Sam, however, knew exactly what he was doing. He was playing to a crowd that liked it rough, rugged, and raw and was not offended by a song like "Feel It." Their attitude was "screw the moral crusaders." They not only knew what "it" was, but challenged Sam to bring it on. Sam likened the sea of people to a hornet's nest right about now, and he patiently waited for the right time to cause a stir.

He followed up with two of his more mainstream hits, "Chain Gang" and "Cupid," downplaying the latter as "a very nice little song," almost as if he doesn't want to appear soft by singing it. He slows the set down by singing the melody from "One More Time," then talks his way into "It's Alright." Again, Sam hasn't broken out the big guns just yet; "It's Alright" missed the charts as the B-side to "Feel It."

He gets the first rise out of the crowd when he breaks into "For Sentimental Reasons," dragging out the "I" in "I've given you my all..." with a hint of that gospel growl the Rev. Charles Cook, Sr. was famous for. He involves the audience in singing the chorus, notching his first female outburst—"oh, yeah, oh, oh"—as a young lady succumbs to Sam's "I love you..." taunting. He has now given the hornet's nest a good poke.

The clock on the wall shows its time to turn up the fire on this party. Sam breaks into the high energy "Twistin' the Night Away," focusing less on the diction clarity of the 45 version and more on the relaxed diction of the street corner version—"look-a-here, let's-a do dat twist!" Sam, always aware and in control, knew just how to talk to his audience to arrive at his desired response. And by the time he summons the gentlemen in the crowd to wave their handkerchiefs in a helicopter motion (*"everybody's* got a handkerchief!"), he's taken a baseball bat to that poor hornet's nest.

With a semi-arrogant warning that he's going to sing all his recent hits, he segues into "Somebody Have Mercy," bringing the second of the Top 10 singles out of his bag, reminding the audience in the meantime that it's not "that leukemia" that requires their mercy. Sam then takes a page out of Papa Cook's Sunday morning book of sermons as he preaches his way into "Bring It On Home to Me." The way Sam deliberately s-s-s-stutters the first word of "Something starts to move..." before cascading into "Home" is vintage Rev. Cook. The crowd is buzzing with excitement now as Sam has assaulted them with a string of back to back to back hits. The next challenge is to seamlessly transition into the Top 10 ballad "Nothin' Can Change This Love" and he does so effectively by turning it into a more up-tempo swing version, getting the audience to join in as well. Finally, Sam concludes with his fifth straight hit "Having a Party," and reminds the audience to "keep having that party" as they sing their way out the door and into the Miami night. The way Sam stirred the hornet's nest this Saturday night was not unlike what Papa did to church congregations on Sunday morning.

If Sam's success in '62 didn't stand for anything else, it marked the year he first "got it." Sam had sought the elusive answer to crossover success ever since releasing "Lovable" some six years earlier, and his English tour was the final affirmation that proved he had indeed come up with the right formula. He was progressively feeding mainstream America doses of black culture through gospel-influenced R&B, and giving a little more of himself with each single. He was subtly stating "I used crossover music just to get my foot in the door. *This* is the real Sam Cooke!" Now that he was in, Sam could sing songs *he* liked, and he sought to push the envelope a little further with the release of the "Live at the Harlem Square" album.

Back in New York, RCA's executives were not having it. They said "thank you, but no thank you" and immediately shot down any thoughts of releasing the live Harlem Square LP. As far as they were concerned, the album had no commercial value; this was a ghetto concert and nothing more. In his heart of hearts Sam knew this project was a long shot and didn't press the issue. He knew they just weren't ready yet. It would take 22 years before RCA would be ready to release "Sam Cooke: Live at the Harlem Square Club, 1963," and this delay may have actually been a blessing in disguise. The 1985 release would attract a whole new generation of Sam Cooke fans broken down into two categories: those who were new to the Sam Cooke experience, and those who had previously dismissed Sam's pop material as being too watered down to consider him a true Soul superstar.

In late February he was back in the studio again, recording Mel Carter's "When a Boy Falls in Love" on Derby Records, a more upscale label Sam had started with Zelda's insistence. Carter had a lilting, high-pitched voice, but Sam was entranced with his talent and had big plans for him in the future. Zelda claims Sam even went so far as to call him his favorite singer in private circles. The single was Derby's first charted hit, rising to #44 pop, #30 R&B. Sam also recorded the song, but it was released as a posthumous single in May of 1965.

Around this same time, Sam went to work on his own LP, "Night Beat," back in RCA's Hollywood studio. The timing of the bluesy album was curious to say the least. Despite all of the chart-busting R&B successes Sam racked up over the past three years, this project almost seemed a regression. The album's setting is supposedly a smoke-filled club after hours, and its intention was to capture the intimate mood of Sam among friends. Isn't this type of album reminiscent of when Sam was trying to establish himself in 1960 rather than after he already had in 1963?

It turns out the album wasn't a regression, but a revisit, although I had to consult Charles in order to get a true understanding of why. He told me that Sam had the type of personality that was bothered by failure and whenever he had a chance to jump back on the horse (e.g. the Copacabana, marriage, etc.), he did. Though 1961's "My Kind of Blues" LP wasn't a failure, Sam knew it wasn't his best effort. I understand and share Sam's dissatisfaction; the album's horn and string arrangements overshadow his unique vocal talent and do nothing to bring us closer to Sam Cooke the artist. It seems that in retrospect, Sam's "My Kind of Blues" was anything but.

"Night Beat" was intended to create the intimacy "My Kind of Blues" failed to provide. This was the best time for Sam to get back on the horse, when he was red-hot and at the pinnacle of his artistic confidence. Once again, Sam's desire to complete a blues album to his satisfaction stemmed from the influence Papa Cook had on his children and the generations under him. It made me search back to two-year old transcripts of two of Papa's grandchildren's describing the way he approached life:

Gene: My grandfather always said "be the best at whatever you do. If you're going to be a janitor, be the best janitor". He would always tell us:

> Once a task has begun,
> Never leave it 'til it's done.
> Be the task great or small,
> Do it well or not at all.

He said "If all they'd allow you to do is dig holes, dig holes so well that everybody in town would say 'now that's the best hole-digger I've seen in my life!'"

Gwen: I think Papa instilled that in all of us. His children, grand-children, his great-grandchildren, this is just the way we are. We're all products of the same seed, and Sam was no different…

"Night Beat" was a result of Sam, either consciously or unconsciously, living out that poem that had been repetitiously drilled into his psyche since childhood. The intimacy "My Kind of Blues" lacked was present in "Night Beat," in large part because of his comfort and confidence with Rene Hall as his arranger. The album contained such gems as "Lost and Lookin'," "Little Red Rooster," "Shake, Rattle and Roll," and the vastly underappreciated "Trouble Blues." Many die-hard Cookies consider "Night Beat" to be Sam's greatest album, but to me it is much more symbolic than just a collection of songs. The album represented Sam's relentless quest for perfection. He often did multiple takes of a song until it met his approval, and, as "Night Beat" showed, he wasn't afraid to revisit a concept that didn't have his complete satisfaction. The album was also significant because it showcased his musical versatility as Sam shifted from a hard-hitting Gospel program, to a jam-packed Soul concert, to an intimate late-night Blues album in successive venues over a two-month span. Most importantly, "Night Beat" helped establish Sam Cooke's artistic virtue by separating him from the pool of less talented singers whose career teetered on the success of their latest single.

For all his time spent performing live in concert, recording albums and overseeing other artists, Sam had yet to release a single in 1963. Finally, in April he came out with the up-tempo "Another Saturday Night," extending his streak of Top 10 R&B singles to seven in a row. The song is about how Sam, the new guy in town, persistently struggles to find a good date. Yeah, right Sam. For all those who knew Sam Cooke well, this song had to be funnier than him trying to teach his girl to dance in 1959's "Everybody Loves to Cha Cha Cha." Apparently enough people were moved by poor Sam's dilemma because "Another Saturday Night" peaked at #10 Pop and gave him his first #1 R&B single since "Twistin' the Night Away" the previous January. I guess it's always good to be able to laugh at your own shortcomings, but it's even better to be able laugh your way to the bank singing about them.

Sam, live in concert, hugged by adoring fans.

(Photo courtesy of Martin Cook)

In the spring of 1963, Sam signed up to headline a national tour that featured the Shirelles and Dionne Warwicke. It was thought that when the tour stopped in Philadelphia, he was introduced to a young business accountant named Allen Klein. In the late 1950's, Klein was rumored to have introduced himself to Bobby Darin as someone who could uncover $100,000 in back royalties from Darin's record label, then delivered the goods. He had earned a reputation among industry insiders as being not only blunt and to the point, but as one who encouraged his clients to walk from a label if the deal wasn't to his satisfaction. To record companies who routinely gouged their artists, he was seen as a threat. To artists inept in spotting accounting irregularities, he was seen as a knight in shining armor.

If Allen Klein had indeed met Sam in Philly in the spring of 1963, it wasn't until later in the year Sam and Klein talked business, and the meeting was arranged at J.W. Alexander's insistence. Allen Klein now stood before Sam promising him the same arrangement he offered Bobby Darin, so sure he could uncover additional royalties due Sam, he offered to audit RCA's ledgers for no charge. Intrigued, Sam shook hands in agreement, not knowing that by doing so he would change his career forever.

Chapter Ten

Establish, Own, and Control:
The Business Side of Sam Cooke

THERE WERE MANY FACETS TO Sam's personality. Fans were aware of his silky smooth voice, his handsome looks, and his suave onstage presence. Off stage, however, there was much more to him than just a pretty face. One of Sam Cooke's most fascinating traits was his refusal to be bullied by anyone, whether it was in a business office or in the back of an alley. I earlier alluded to the time he spent with the Soul Stirrers as being beneficial in honing his business sense, but an equal amount of credit should be given to his Bronzeville background for honing his street sense.

Before one gets the wrong impression, let me define what I mean by street sense. So many times, the phrase carries negative connotations of pimps, gangsters, hustlers, and drug dealers. Indeed, the ability to deal with these elements is part of what defines street sense. But there's also an innate survivability aspect which, when combined effectively with raw determination and business foresight, can yield much more powerful results than your average university MBA.

Starting in the mid-'90's and extending through the new century, for example, America has seen the rise of the enterprising hip-hop mogul. Entertainers such as Sean "P. Diddy" Combs and Percy "Master P" Miller gained recognition not just as flamboyant artists, but as extremely successful businessmen as well. They combined business acumen with a raw desire to succeed, and regardless of the odds against them, stormed into the boardrooms of corporate America refusing to take "no" for an answer. They weren't your prototypical businessmen, but this unique quality worked to their advantage. Combs and Miller found they could relate to the hip-hop community in ways in which a "suit" could not, and as a result managed to carve their niche in a multi-billion dollar industry. Regardless of your personal feelings toward them, both men owned several legitimate companies and were worth well over $300 million before their 35th birthdays. They *made* themselves into young forces to be reckoned with.

Sam was that enterprising mogul and young force to be reckoned with as well; he just happened to do it 30 years before the gentlemen listed above. Not only was he the first black artist to become a major player in the recording industry, it was *because* he paved the way for the Sean Combses and Percy Millers their success was even imaginable. And the list doesn't stop with just Combs and Miller. You could also add Russell Simmons, Andre "Dr. Dre" Young, Shawn "Jay-Z" Carter and O'Shea "Ice Cube" Jackson to the growing number of successful hip-hop CEO's. In fact all of the gentlemen listed above have branched off into other avenues such as clothing lines, acting, and film production, but it was all because one man broke the glass ceiling. That man was Sam Cooke.

Since Sam was from a different era, his survivability sense manifested itself in different ways. Sam had to endure the racial prejudices of the 50's and 60's, and it was this survivability instinct that gave him the tenacity to carry on. He was the first black performer to refuse to sing to segregated audiences, not only risking his career, but his life as well. Sam recognized that the lion's share of the industry's profits went not to the artist, but to those behind the scenes, so he took great strides to establish and maintain ownership of his career. Sam Cooke paved the way for the modern artist to be successful both on stage and in the boardroom, and he deserves this recognition in music history.

Sam was able to open the doors he opened because he didn't walk around with his chin on his chest. He had an edge, an air of confidence, so much so that when he said something you knew he meant business. The tone he spoke with wasn't anger, but it was universally recognizable and it instantly said "I'm not to be messed with." My uncles David, Charles, and L.C. have a similar tone, and it all descended from Papa Cook. When Papa spoke, whether in the pulpit or just telling a story, he had the type of voice that captivated your undivided attention, but if you made him angry, you knew immediately you'd pissed off the wrong person. Sam was just an extension of that same bloodline.

"Sam stood up for what he believed in," Agnes states boldly. "He did

not back down. In one situation (Little Rock, 1958) he had a show and
they wanted him to do two shows, one for the blacks and one for the
whites. He said 'absolutely not.' He had contracted to do one show and
that's all he was going to do. They still weren't satisfied with this so what
they did was sit the whites on one side and the blacks on the other. He
really wanted all of his audience to be together. He said 'If this is the way
they want to play the game, I'm going to teach them a lesson.' When he
went out on stage, he sang that entire night facing the black audience and
he did not turn to the white audience at all. He said 'I'll fulfill my contract, but they can't tell me which way to turn and sing.' The next time he
went back, everyone sat together. He believed in standing up for what he
felt was right. Once his mind was set on something, then that was it."

"One time in Memphis (1961), we were staying at the Lorraine Motel,"
Charles recalls. "Sam sent me ahead to the auditorium because he was
told they were trying to segregate the audience. They were seating the
whites on the main floor and even though there were empty seats, the
blacks had to sit upstairs in the balcony. I went back and told Sam. Sam
said 'Forget it, then. Crain, cancel the show.' Then the police came and
threatened to take our cars because Sam didn't perform. Sam told the police 'Y'all ain't taking nothin'. As a matter of fact, y'all better not touch my
cars!' Now, I was gonna go move the cars and Sam said 'Man, don't move
nothin'. Ain't nobody gonna bother my cars.' And they didn't. They had to
refund everybody's money and we went on to the next town."

I was always amazed at the way Sam never held anything back, espe-
cially in the 50's and 60's when blacks were expected to "know their place."
In a lot of instances where the normal black man would've held his tongue,
Sam didn't care. He didn't have a "place" as far as he was concerned.

"I remember your grandmother went to the William Morris Agency
with Sam in New York," David retells the story, "and Sam was upset because they hadn't been booking him. 'I don't need to pay you fuckers 10%
and Crain is getting all the bookings! Y'all ain't making me! Crain is getting all my bookings! What do I need to give you fuckers 10% for if that's
the case?' Sam would cuss them out, now!"

"Would he? Even at William Morris?" I asked.

"Any of them!" Charles shouted.

"Hell, yeah!" David agreed. "William Morris, RCA…"

At RCA he constantly found it necessary to re-establish the respect that should've been given an artist of his stature.

"Sam went into RCA and they had Elvis Presley's pictures all over the wall of the lobby," Charles recalls. "Damn near every picture was Elvis. Sam told them 'look here, the next time I come in here, my pictures better be up there, too, or y'all can find somebody else!' And when he came back, believe me, they had his pictures up there!"

"And he was never one to back down?" I asked.

"I'm telling you, Erik, man, Sam didn't mess around," David says, shaking his head to emphasize his point. "Sam didn't take no shit from nobody. Back in St. Louis, right before Eddie Cunningham got killed, Sam's dressing room at the Sportsman's Club was in the basement so Sam sent Eddie to go get some ice for the drinks."

"But Eddie and one of these big bouncers had gotten into an argument and he hit Eddie in the head with butt of a gun. Eddie came back to the dressing room holding his head with one hand and the empty bucket with the other. Sam said 'Man, what happened to you?' Eddie said 'I went to go get the ice and this dude told me I couldn't get no ice and hit me upside the head.' So Sam went out to talk to him, the dude said something smart and Boom! Sam threw him up against the wall, just like that! That's when Oopy (Traveler's bass singer, George McCurn) leaned over and whispered to the guy 'You're messing with that man's bread and butter!' This big bouncer was steady apologizing, scared to death, 'I'm sorry! I'm sorry, Sam! I didn't know he worked for you!'"

"I remember one time he wanted the President of RCA-Victor to come to his show in Atlantic City," Charles kicks in. "He was all excited; he had reserved a table down in the front for him and everything. Well, they sent a Vice President down and man, Sam was pissed. He wouldn't even let the guy explain why the President didn't show. He told the guy 'I don't talk to flunkeys. Get the fuck outta here. Tell (the President) if he's not here tomorrow night, you can forget about me.' The next night, if you look out in the audience, who do you think was at the front table? The President of RCA-Victor, that's who. Sam did <u>not</u> play."

Before Sam signed with RCA, they had one Pop superstar, Elvis Presley. After that, there was a tremendous drop-off between Elvis and their second selling artist. One of the reasons RCA agreed to Sam's unique contract was that they were aware he had the potential to fill that void, which he did successfully. Sam was always conscious of the fact he was a major moneymaker for RCA, and he demanded they recognize his importance to the label the same way they did Elvis Presley's. This demand for respect held true for his other business entities as well. In a separate interview, Agnes and Gene remembered this about Sam:

Agnes: Sam once contacted William Morris (Agency) and told them he wanted to do a TV sing-along. They told him that idea would never work, that it wouldn't go over with the public, they wouldn't accept it. He wanted to sing with the audience on TV, sort of like he did (in concert) with "If I Had a Hammer." They told him it wouldn't work.

Gene: Then a few months later, Variety magazine ran an ad saying William Morris was sponsoring a show with Mitch Miller doing a sing-along with the audience, and that the people at home could sing along with the words on their television. But this was after they told Sam it would never work. They told him "it works fine in your shows, but America's not going to sing along with you on TV."

Agnes: And that's when he fired them, when they took his idea and gave it to somebody else. But remember, that was during the 60's and that's how they did blacks...

That very well may have been the way they did blacks in the '60's, but that excuse didn't hold water with Sam Cooke. Sam was unique in that he didn't always see people in terms of black and white, even though he was living in a society that clearly did. As a black man, he felt he was entitled to the same treatment as everyone else. As a major recording star, he felt he was entitled to the same respect as any white artist of his caliber.

Sam enjoyed highly successful gospel and pop careers and his record labels and publishing company were doing well, yet he constantly felt like a second class citizen and it tormented him to no end. Here was Sam Cooke, an international star with millions of records sold and even more adoring fans, still ignored at Southern diners while white patrons were seated before him. He constantly found himself relegated to "Colored Only" motels in certain parts of the country even though he had enough money to *buy* most of the motels that called for his exclusion. He took great pains to make sure he carried himself with class, pride and dignity yet he constantly had to demand the respect that he should've been granted naturally. He felt that all of his years of sacrifice should have paid off in more than just material items. It should've opened the same doors that it did for others who hadn't had to work nearly as hard for nearly as long. Sam fought tooth and nail to grasp the top rung, only to come up with a handful of air. What more could he do? With a sense of despair, he realized that despite all his life's accomplishments, he was still seen as a nigger in the eyes of most Americans.

What bothered Sam most was his inability to be able to break into the upper-echelon venues. While he loved performing before "his people," whether it were singing gospel or pop, he knew that there was another level of entertainment where the work was less taxing and the rewards were more substantial. He was older now and he'd seen how the road could wear down an entertainer and he didn't want that to be his fate. One of the reasons he had spent so much time and effort developing his businesses was that he realized he would need something to fall back on if he ever decided he wanted to stay home full time. There was more to life than hopping from town to town doing one-nighters. He wanted the top supper clubs. He wanted a run in Las Vegas. Didn't he deserve this? By mid-1963 Elvis Presley had starred in a dozen films. Hadn't Sam Cooke paid his dues to the point where he could see *his* name in lights?

Sam live in concert on the "Chitlin' Circuit."

(Photo courtesy of Charlene Graham)

As if he had been summoned by Sam's despair—poof!—Allen Klein magically appeared as Sam's genie, claiming he could make Sam's every wish come true. He told Sam he could get him the respect he deserved from RCA in the form of a new contract. He told Sam he could recover monies owed to him from the time he signed his present deal. And finally he hit the jackpot by promising Sam Cooke what he valued more than anything else—another shot at the Copa. Allen Klein in a business negotiation was a lot like Sam Cooke performing on stage: he knew just what buttons to push to get the desired results.

Orphaned as a child before being taken in by an aunt, Allen Klein discovered his affinity for math and accounting as a young man. He worked several odd jobs before settling in at a company whose responsibilities, among others, involved handling the bookkeeping duties for several celebrities. It was there he studied the subtle nuances of the bookkeeping business and how easy it was to find accounting mistakes in corporate audits. Once he went into business for himself, Klein would often impress potential clients with the amount of information he knew about their music and financial situation. If the old saying was true that first impressions last, then Allen Klein always did his homework in order to make sure he'd win clients over from the first handshake.

At the time Klein met Sam in 1963, he was still relatively new in the entertainment business, but his reputation grew as his client list grew. After Bobby Darin most of his clients were up and coming artists like the future Rockabilly Hall of Fame guitarist Buddy Knox. Klein's brutal honesty and penchant for profanity was a turn-off for some (he was known to have been kicked out of meetings for swearing too much), but nearly everyone he came in contact with could tell he was an extremely intelligent individual. What Klein would do was use the promise of finding unpaid royalties as a lost leader. His true goal was to go from auditing the artist's books as their accountant to controlling their books as their business manager. It wasn't until the post-Sam Cooke era he would gain his most fame (or infamy) via business deals with the Beatles and the Rolling Stones.

In 1965, for example, he was able to secure the Rolling Stones a $1.4 million royalty advance which they thought would be deposited into their account, Nanker Phlege Music, Ltd. Instead, Klein allegedly deposited the money into an account he had set up and owned himself–Nanker Phlege Music, *Inc*. In a move that wouldn't be discovered for years to come, Allen Klein had taken advantage of a clause in his contract with the Stones which said he had a full twenty years to pay them the $1.4 million principal. Any interest accrued in the meantime would belong to Klein. The Rolling Stones also claimed they thought they owned their highly-valued publishing rights when in fact they had mistakenly signed them over to Klein's company of a similar name. In May of 1972, the Rolling Stones dissolved all ties with Allen Klein, but not before filing a lawsuit against Klein and his ABKCO label for $29 million.

In 1966 Allen Klein tried unsuccessfully to "buy" the Beatles from their manager at the time, Brian Epstein. But it wasn't until 1969, when John Lennon hired him as his manager, did he crack his way inside the band. He eventually went on to manage George Harrison and Ringo Starr, but Paul McCartney heeded the warnings of Rolling Stone Mick Jagger and didn't sign with Klein. Years later, after Lennon put two and two together, he realized that he had been purposely targeted by Allen Klein. It seems Klein had gradually felt out members of the Rolling Stones as to who ran what inside the Beatle camp, and then approached John Lennon. Lennon, Harrison and Starr would all end up suing Allen Klein in 1973. Six years later Klein would be sent to prison for tax evasion violations stemming from mismanagement of the Beatles' company, Apple Corps, and Paul McCartney went so far as to publicly blame Allen Klein for the Beatles' breakup. Their legendary *Abbey Road* album contains a personal shot at Allen Klein called "You Never Give Me Your Money," as if it were written from Klein's perspective. Ray Davies of The Kinks was once quoted as saying "I never signed a piece of paper with Klein, but I'm sure he can pull one out of a drawer!"

Before the Rolling Stones and before the Beatles, however, there was Sam Cooke. In fact, one of Klein's strongest selling points with both groups was that he had been Sam Cooke's manager, fully aware both the Stones and the Beatles admired and respected Sam's work.

In a 1971 Playboy interview, Allen Klein described Sam as a great artist and songwriter that "had no money" when they met. If anything, Sam represented the antithesis of the average artist; he reaped publishing royalties through his lucrative record deal, was a tour headliner that commanded top dollar, and owned record labels that returned handsome profits. Sam was doing quite well financially after signing with RCA in 1960, despite Klein's exaggerated claim to the contrary. Sam had enough business sense to recognize he deserved a better contract than his Keen contract, and successfully negotiated one that met his demands years before he ever met Klein. While Sam may not have been receiving all he was due, he certainly wasn't in dire financial straits that required immediate rescue.

Another exaggerated claim of Allen Klein's seems to be the $100,000 in back royalties he supposedly found auditing Bobby Darin's record label. In "Dream Boogie," author Peter Guralnick alleges that Klein's meeting with Atlantic Records "led to both a financial windfall and, indirectly, to Darin's leaving Atlantic for Capitol."

First of all, Bobby Darin recorded his biggest hits "Splish Splash," "Dream Lover," and "Mack the Knife" not on Atlantic Records, but its subsidiary label, Atco. He left Atco Records for Capitol Records in 1962. Secondly, according to Darin's former manager Steve Blauner, "Allen Klein did do an audit for us, and turned up practically nothing. The relationship with Klein was a disaster. It had nothing to do with Bobby's split from Atco." Blauner, through Bobby Darin archivist Jimmy Scalia added "Everything in ("Dream Boogie") about Darin is erroneous. All of Klein's interaction was with me, not Bobby Darin. The worst thing that Sam Cooke did was meet Klein. He is single-handedly responsible for Cooke not getting his due."

To Allen Klein's credit, his business relationship with Sam started off on a more successful note than the one with Bobby Darin. Within months after meeting Sam, Klein found almost $150,000 in unpaid royalties, plus inked a new RCA contract for $500,000 payable over a three-year period. Though the signing bonus may seem miniscule by today's standards, in 1963 it was in historic in that it marked the largest advance ever given to a black artist. Soon after the new contract, J. W. Alexander convinced Sam to reduce Jess Rand's duties and take on Allen Klein as his manager, though the two never signed a formal contract.

Later that year Tracey Ltd. (named after Sam's daughter) was incorporated and unbeknownst to Sam, created the duo's first discrepancy. Tracey Ltd. was a production company designed to protect its owner against taxes. All of his songs released by RCA would filter through Tracey first and Sam would withdraw money from Tracey as needed. On paper, the idea was ingenious—Sam would become his own self-contained company by being able to write, record, publish and manufacture his own music. RCA's role would be to serve as the distributor of Sam's records.

But who exactly owned Tracey? According to Daniel Wolff's "You Send Me," State of Nevada records showed that Tracey listed Sam as President, J.W. Alexander as Vice President, and Klein as secretary. What the Articles of Incorporation didn't show was that the company was fully owned by Allen Klein. By all family accounts however, Tracey Limited's original incorporation listed Sam as President and sole owner, J.W. Alexander as Vice President and his *father*, Charles Cook, Sr., as Secretary, far different than the order of incorporation Wolff found on file with the Secretary of State in Nevada.

Contrary to popular belief, Sam wasn't totally mesmerized by Allen Klein's charm and business savvy, nor did he blindly give Klein free reign amongst his business affairs. Not only did Sam note the apprehension close associates like S.R. Crain had about going into business with Klein, Sam shared much of the same concerns. It had been years since Sam had called Bronzeville home, but his ability to detect a person's ulterior motives was a trait he acquired growing up in Chicago's tough streets and was one that had never left him. He was aware Klein's take-charge attitude could present a problem, and though the Beatle and Rolling Stone incidences would occur years down the road, Sam had the presence of mind to take precautions of his own. Sam chose Papa to be a figure-head officer so that no matter what happened in the future, he would always have controlling interest in Tracey. "One thing about Sam," Dot observed from their many years together, "He was smart. He kept his eyes open, his ears open. He didn't let people take complete advantage." The way Sam saw it, he needed Klein for two things—to negotiate his deal at RCA and to get him another booking at the Copacabana. Beyond that, Sam would have no use for Klein and planned to sever their relationship when he felt the time was right.

When I requested an archival search from Nevada's Office of the Secretary of State in August of 2004, I specifically asked for the list of officers for Tracey Limited. They sent me a letter confirming that Tracey Limited was registered on October 4, 1963, but the list of incorporating officers could no longer be found. An excerpt of the letter I received reads as follows:

Generally we also provide a copy of the last listing of officers, which are required annually. In this instance, I am unable to provide you with any such information, as the original microfiche are simply not in the appropriate files. All of the pertinent information is there while the actual documentation is not.

Perhaps the best person to address Tracey's ownership would be my cousin Gene. Even though he was just fourteen when Sam died, his father, Agnes' first husband Eddie Jamison, investigated Sam's death for years. Eddie was a Public Administrator for the City of Chicago and shared his findings with Gene over the years until dying unexpectedly of a massive heart attack in March of 2002:

"My dad worked for the Office of Public Administration and he was in charge of finding the next of kin whenever there was a death without a will. The Public Administrator's Office comes in, seals up the property, inventories it all and sees that their belongings get to the proper person. If no next of kin can be found, everything reverts back to the state. He was accustomed to finding corporation papers and finding out when they were filed, who filed them, how to read them, and so on. Investigating assets was his bread and butter, though. Safe deposit boxes, bank accounts…if they existed, my father could find them."

"The family asked him to trace Sam (after his death in 1964), to see what he could find out. Papa knew that Sam had told him he was on the Board of Directors. He was wondering where these papers were and what was happening with the company (Tracey, Ltd.). At that point Barbara was saying there was no will, no nothing. When my dad started researching how Sam set up SAR, Malloy, KAGS, and Tracey, he found the original papers, but what he found was all different. The paperwork was different from what Sam had originally set up and had told people he originally set up. The more he dug, the more he found out, the closer he got to parties that didn't want to be discovered. He got a couple of phone calls telling him to mind his own business. They said 'stay out of things that don't concern you, you're not even married to the Cook sister any more. We know where those two children you have go to school, and we know where you are, so mind your own business.'"

"But after that, every now and then he would get a little curious and sneak and do a little something even though they told him not to. He may have gotten a reply to something he had put out earlier, maybe five of six years before, and he would check it out. It was an ongoing thing. Whenever he found something that would pique his curiosity he checked into it. Also, years after they quote, unquote, "scared him off," he started looking again, especially when the rumors surfaced that Sam's proceeds from his catalog was being sold, so he started a little bit of digging then. There were a lot of roadblocks tossed in his way but he found everything had been taken over by ABKCO."

"He found documents that suggested Sam wanted things done one way, and later found what was on file at the time of his investigation was totally different. Like any corporation, your board votes on different things and as many people you can get on your side, the better. Sam, naturally, always made sure it was set up for him to be the winner. Papa was just a vote, just a figurehead. At some point Papa was removed, and a few other changes later, Sam was no longer in control of the company. Not only did he lose sole ownership of the company, he wasn't the controlling partner, either. Sam had made a lot of sacrifices and suddenly all of that was wiped out, undone. And something he swore would never happen, happened. Someone else owned it, and its not that we're bigots or anything, but a white man owned it, and he said he never wanted that to happen. His point of view was that the entertainment business for so many years used black talent, or rather *misused* black talent, and the powers that be got rich while the black entertainer with all the talent got almost nothing. Sam was determined that would never happen to him. There's no way he'd knowingly set up anything so that anyone owned him but him."

My Aunt Agnes specifically remembers Eddie Jamison confirming the fact that Papa was indeed an officer of the company. This took me back to an earlier excerpt from a conversation about how passionate Sam felt about being in control of his music.

"Back when Mama was living on 83rd," Agnes recalled, "me and Sam stayed up until 2 o'clock in the morning and Sam told me, 'You know what? Some nights I get on that stage and I sweat. I look up and I've lost as much as 4 pounds during one performance. And I'll be damned if I let a white man get rich off of my sweat.' But he did."

The name and post-office address of each of the first

Board of Directors are as follows:

NAME	ADDRESS
Sam Cooke	6425 Hollywood Blvd., Hollywood, Calif.
James Alexander	1845 S. Andrews Place, Los Angeles, Calif.
S. R. Crain	4526 Woodlawn Ave., Chicago, Ill.
Rev. Charles S. Cooke	Chicago, Ill.

Tracey Limited's Articles of Incorporation *Board of Directors page, as filed October 4, 1963. This document was located in a subsequent search.*

No one in the family can say for sure how the officers ended up so radically different from Sam's wishes, but one thing is certain: Sam would have <u>never</u> knowingly agreed to an arrangement which took artistic control, especially control of the KAGS catalog, out of his hands. In contract negotiations for a major record deal, he put his career on the line by holding steadfast to the demand he retain control of his copyrights. Why would he freely sign that right away? Not to mention, why would Sam make a special point of naming the company after his daughter if he never intended to be the sole owner?

J.W. Alexander was the one who actually registered the corporation in Nevada, so he at least was aware of how the final list of officers read. And as co-owner of SAR Records and KAGS Music Publishing, any change of officers could have been done with his approval and the not-heavily-scrutinized signature of one of the other owners, Sam Cooke or S. R. Crain. I found it very interesting that the only information missing from the State of Nevada's archives is the list of incorporating officers. If it weren't for the research of Daniel Wolff and G. David Tenenbaum years earlier, the list, like many other important facts surrounding Sam's death and business affairs, may have been lost forever. Whatever the case, the family is convinced Sam took precautions to protect his business interests, despite the fact that Tracey Records is currently a division of Allen Klein's ABKCO Records.

Chapter Eleven

Tribulation to Triumph II: The Return to the *Copacabana*

THE CASUAL OBSERVER COULD'VE EASILY written Sam Cooke off as another late-night party hound who lifted more skirts than a Santa Ana wind. They could've focused only on the way his suave personality, movie star looks and flashy smile screamed "ladies man" as he entered a room. In the superficial world of Hollywood, it would be only natural to look at Sam's fame, wealth, and his love for the finer things in life and add him to the pile of shallow actors and entertainers who lived only for themselves and for their careers. Player, Playboy, or plastic, the casual observer could have melted Sam's persona into any one of these stereotypes, but by doing so, they would have mistakenly prejudged what it really was that made Sam Cooke tick.

While Sam fit into his L.A. lifestyle rather seamlessly, the designer clothes, secluded house, and imported luxury cars were just material symbols of his recording success. Truth be told, he was still a transplant, and his Midwestern roots and values were never more evident as in his attitude toward his immediate and extended families. I'm not going to paint a picture of Sam as the traditional family man—with seven children by five different women, it would be impossible to do so—but he did grow up with a strong emphasis on the family unit. Sam's parents had been married almost 40 years and despite the fact Papa Cook had spent a good part of that time on the road as a traveling preacher, the marriage remained strong. The Cooks never had a lot of money, but Papa always managed to protect and provide for not only his family, but for the kids in the neighborhood who found themselves in need of a hot meal or safe haven. By the same token, Sam's mother always stressed the importance of attending the Cook family picnics in July as well as sitting down together for Thanksgiving dinner. She felt it was important the whole family unite, even if it were only twice a year. The Cook household was one built around love, and you didn't have to be born a Cook to recognize that fact. Charles' ex-wife Phyllis, for example, had an interesting initial response after hearing of my plans to write a book on Sam's life:

"What I'd like to see you talk about is the closeness of the family. There was a tremendous amount of love and closeness in the Cook family. When people talk about family memories, they're not always good. I've actually seen people fight at family reunions. There are usually some hostilities somewhere, but you didn't find them in this family. Sam, as well as all of the Cook children, came from a strong man and strong woman that instilled that kind of love. It wasn't just Sam that sang, everybody did, but because he pursued it further, they all supported him. Nobody was jealous or tried to backbite or talk about him. Whatever he needed, they were there for support. I think that's a good story, because it's not the common story. Take a look at how Marvin Gaye's family fought and how his life ended. I still to this day talk about the closeness of the Cook family."

Sam cherished the sanctity of being able to come home, if for no other reason to clear his head from the rigors of being an entertainer and businessman. He enjoyed being around people who loved him for what he was, and not who he was. He also loved the joy and excitement his return to Chicago would bring, especially when he could see the faces of his young nieces and nephews as he showered them with gifts:

"I'll never forget the Christmas he bought me some little high heel shoes and a little stole," Renee remembers. "I didn't know any better, I thought it was real mink! I walked around the house in my shoes and my stole and wouldn't take them off for anyone! It's just those little things that are so memorable to me."

"Sam gave me a string of pearls for my high school graduation," my mother recalls. "He told me 'a lady should never be without a string of pearls in her jewelry box.' This gift meant so much to me because as a young girl I was always conscious of my dark skin, but in my uncle's eyes, I was a lady. I cried because it was so uplifting for my delicate self esteem, and I still have that same string of pearls to this very day."

"My mother and father were both family oriented, and they instilled in us 'all for one and one for all'," Agnes would say. Sam knew that if the fame and fortune were to leave him tomorrow, his family, especially his parents, brothers and sisters, would always be there. As a result, his family's well-being came before everything else, and it was his family, not the parties he attended or the material items he could buy, that he cherished most.

Quite naturally, Sam wanted to duplicate that same sanctity in his own household. Life as an entertainer meant constantly being in the public eye, so when Sam came home he just wanted to be a husband to his wife and a father to his children. The reason he wanted to sing the Las Vegas circuit or the high-end supper clubs was so that he could be there more as a father and spend less time on the road. When he did tour, Barbara and the kids would sometimes accompany him or at least meet him in certain cities along the way. A person with as many irons in the fire as Sam Cooke had to steal quality family time wherever he could.

Though his marriage was far from perfect, Sam felt that as a father there was so much he could give his children. He could afford to send them to the best schools. They could travel the world together and Sam could show them far away places he hadn't had a chance to see as a child. Sam had started to show greater interest in black history and became more conscious of the impact the Civil Rights movement had on black Americans. His bookshelves were filled with books on black history and he would raise his children to be proud and aware of their African heritage, and that they didn't have to blindly accept what was given to them. Sam wanted to one day be able to devote most of his time to his children, but for now he knew that the greatest gift he could give Linda, Tracey, and Vincent was the same gift of love he had received as a child.

Faces of Tracey: (a), (b) in Detroit at age 3, September 1963, (c) at home in California at age 12, August, 1972, (d) in Chicago at age 15, August 1975.

(Detroit photos courtesy of Toni Cook Howard, others courtesy of Gwendolyn Greene)

Sam's challenge was finding a way to be an effective dad when he couldn't be home, and he focused on establishing household rules in his absence. For example, Tracey's brush with death the summer before called for strict enforcement of swimming pool guidelines. The pool sat at the front of the house, just to the right of the double-door entrance and behind the main gate. Sam explicitly instructed Barbara to cover the pool when it wasn't being used. If she wasn't able to do it, the maid or the gardener were supposed to see to it the pool was covered. At any rate, there would be no excuse for any more close calls like the one they had before.

That being said, when Sam was interrupted by a phone call at SAR's offices on Monday, June 17, 1963, you can imagine his horror and disbelief at hearing the news his 18 month-old son Vincent had accidentally fallen into the pool. The story Sam later told his brothers and sisters was that Tracey and Vincent were playing in the pool area when they began a tug-o-war over a toy teddy bear. Vincent pulled away, falling backwards into the pool. Tracey immediately ran into the house to tell Barbara, but Barbara couldn't understand her three-year old's animated pleas. By the time she realized what Tracey was trying to say, it was too late. Meanwhile, Sam rushed home from the office, but didn't arrive until after the paramedics had given up. For several minutes he held his lifeless son poolside as the toy bear floated innocently on the water's surface.

In his mind Sam tried to make sense of the situation. He knew the family had been using the pool over the weekend, partially explaining why it hadn't been covered, but one glaring fact prevailed: both children had been left unsupervised. Sam could not fathom how a mother could allow her two small children to be put in such a predicament not once, but twice. He spent long hours on the phone with Papa, seeking the one voice of reason which always seemed to bring him comfort. Papa explained God's will and how man's faith was continually tested throughout the Bible, yet man was always strengthened in the end. Sam told Papa that he believed Barbara hadn't responded immediately to Tracey's pleas, which hurt him more than anything. He had noticed that Barbara had become less and less attentive to situations around her, and that she had to constantly be reminded of mundane tasks like covering the pool. Papa told Sam to pray for strength, but it seemed that when Vincent died, something inside Sam died as well. He stayed legally married to Barbara for the remaining year and a half of his life, but emotionally he divorced himself from her that fateful summer day.

"Sam told me he told Barbara 'do not let the children in the yard unless the pool was covered,'" Agnes recalls about the incident. "He had emphasized that to her so many times. The yard was gated, they couldn't get out, but he was worried about the pool."

For the next several months Sam was just a shell of his usual self. His bubbly, outgoing personality was gone and he now found comfort in spending long periods of time alone. In his solitude he tried to rationalize how all of this could have come to pass. As the man of the house, Sam knew he was supposed to be the protector. He didn't see to it the pool was covered that morning, and now young Vincent was gone. But try as he might to carry the entire burden of responsibility, he kept replaying the scene in his mind of his desperate daughter pleading to her unresponsive mother. Sam's demeanor grew dark, cold and distant, and as he brooded, he started to drink more than usual. In Sam's mind, he felt Barbara was the one responsible for Vincent's death and he never forgave her for her negligence.

During Sam's bereavement period, RCA quietly released two singles. The first one, "Cool Train," dropped in July of 1963 and was historic in two ways. For starters, it marked the first time a Sam Cooke single was released in stereo. Unfortunately, it also was the first time one of his A-sides hadn't charted since "Feel It" had fallen short nearly two years before. "Cool Train" had been sitting on the shelf at RCA, then mercilessly pressed into service to keep Sam's music in radio rotations. Sam's performance on "Cool Train" was less than his usual high standards, a fact that apparently didn't sneak past his true fans. Sam did strike gold on the flipside, however. "Frankie and Johnny," recorded two years earlier, peaked at #14 pop and #4 R&B.

In October, RCA followed up with the release of the Willie Dixon classic "Little Red Rooster" with "You Gotta Move" on the flipside. Both songs were from Sam's "Night Beat" album recorded that February and "Rooster" was blues-oriented much like "Cool Train." The difference between the two was that Sam's performance on "Little Red Rooster" was top notch and the listening audience responded accordingly, pushing the single to #11 pop and #7 R&B. In the period from January of 1962 through the end of 1963, Sam had had eight singles peak in the top twenty on the pop charts and nine go #7 or higher (eight of those in the top 5) on the R&B charts. The fact that his last two charting singles were "recycled" showed the strength of his popularity as an entertainer and the depth of his talent as an artist.

To keep himself busy and his mind off of the loss of his son, Sam collaborated with New Orleans musician Harold Battiste to organize the first of a series of urban "Soul Workshops" meant to serve as mini audition posts for up-and-coming singers and musicians. Sam envisioned a meeting place in which artists of similar musical and cultural backgrounds could feed off of each other's talents in a comfortable surrounding. He bought the recording equipment and set up the first Workshop in a rented storefront in the heart of L.A.'s black community. The concept of the Soul Workshop was a further extension of Sam's growing awareness that black promoters needed an outlet in which they could get the first crack at evaluating raw talent, an outlet other than Hollywood record company offices. The idea was as political as it was artistic, and though the Workshops never really got off the ground, they were a glimpse of the pioneering path Sam had in mind for black music. The thought of successful Soul Workshops caused record company executives to squirm in their seats and take notice that Sam Cooke's foresight and vision threatened the very fiber of their industry's profitability.

Record company executives weren't the only one taking notice of Sam Cooke. In those days, a good percentage of black recording artists with only *half* of Sam's success were being extorted on a regular basis. For example, a black star that shall remain nameless died after many years of extortion, and the next-in-line black artist on his label was immediately told he was expected to continue a similar arrangement. It was understood in the record business this was just the way things operated. Yet here was Sam Cooke, a major recording star that owned his own record labels and music publishing companies, repeatedly ignoring his "duty" to do the same. Quite naturally, Sam's actions were viewed as blatantly disrespectful to those who felt they were owed a piece of the action.

Sam's refusal to go along with the status quo was undoubtedly instrumental in his ability to accomplish unprecedented goals, but I also wondered if his defiance could have been detrimental in the long run. Since there have always been rumors of Sam's death being mob-related, in an interview with David and Charles, I candidly asked Charles if he felt any of the mob theories had validity. The frankness of his response caught me off guard:

"I'll tell you what. They sent people to try to talk to Sam, and Sam didn't give a damn. Sam said 'Fuck 'em.' He said 'I ain't thinkin' about them motherfuckers. Ain't nobody gonna tell me what to do.'"

The casual mood of our conversation darkened immediately. Even after 40 years the topic was so sensitive and so intensely emotional, Charles found it painful to elaborate in this and in subsequent interviews. There was a long silence between the three of us, all thinking separately but thinking the same thing: the take-no-mess attitude which built Sam's wealth and made him the music pioneer he was could've possibly been what led to his downfall. Sam Cooke changed the way the game had been played. He was the first black artist to make a major record company comply with *his* terms. Atlantic Records refused to give in to his demand that he own the rights to his songs, consequently Sam signed a deal with a label that would. In addition, he tried to convince other artists to rise up and take similar control of their destinies. Between his refusal to "pay the piper" and his constant attempts to break away from the Hollywood traditions in place for decades, there's no doubt his power and obstinacy ruffled more than a few feathers.

What was also surprising was that there was a major black recording artist and at least one white silver screen star urging Sam to go along with the program. Both of them called Sam repeatedly and stressed the fact that "these people mean business," but Sam refused to give in. Besides, one reason Sam hired Allen Klein was because of Klein's influence outside the boardroom. Klein's industry reputation was so well respected that he could keep the "small dogs," as Sam used to call them, at bay. However, as the months passed, their persistence grew greater and greater and their threats more serious.

As the calendar year rolled over, Sam began 1964 with one focus: returning to New York City's Copacabana. Just like Sam's car accident five years earlier, Vincent's death had been the spark Sam needed to jumpstart his efforts on taking his career to the next level. Now, more than ever, he wanted to pursue high-class clientele, and he knew that in order to do so he'd have to learn how to master the sophisticated supper club audience just as he had mastered the gospel and pop audiences. Sam hadn't forgotten the humbling experience the Copa dished out in 1958, and vowed to never go through that same humiliation again. Sam approached a second run at the Copa as a prizefighter, stripped of his championship belt, would approach a rematch. He'd prepare and prepare and prepare, and when he finally thought he was ready, he'd prepare some more.

Sam returned to the studios and released "Ain't that Good News/Basin Street" in January of 1964 and the A-side steamrolled to #11 across both charts. It seems, however, Sam spent most of his time between January and July concentrating on the Copa instead of focusing on his business affairs. Not-so-subtle changes were taking place behind the scenes during this period. Zelda Sands, for example, remembers how Allen Klein began to exert his influence throughout Sam's enterprises. Johnnie Morisette's contract had been dropped in May, and there were major internal conflicts she wasn't comfortable talking about, but she vividly recalls Klein's attempt to take over Mel Carter's management without Carter's blessing. The young singer, rattled by Klein's audacity, secretly called Zelda and asked her would she be his manager. Klein found out about the conversation and angrily forced Zelda to choose between running SAR's office and managing Mel Carter. The choice she made ended her four year tenure at

SAR. "I took Mel with me," Zelda says. "Sam let him out of his contract and I ended up managing him for 26 ½ years. 'Told Me, Thrill Me, Kiss Me' is still one of the top oldies of all time. "

Meanwhile, Sam was working feverishly to prepare for the Copa. After months of hand-picking songs and arrangements, his advisors (Klein, Alexander, and club-set veteran Buddy Howe) decided it would be best to test out his act in upstate New York the weekend before the Copa. Once again, Sam turned his back on his successful string of self-penned R&B hits and concentrated on show tunes and folk classics, but despite months of rehearsal, the first night in the Catskills was a disaster. Usually at home on a stage, Sam ended up having flashbacks of his previous Copa experience and at one point abandoned his play list, leaving his band in a state of bewilderment and disarray.

That night, Sam and his consultants—including friend and former William Morris agent, Jerry Brandt—went back to the drawing board. They realized they needed the expertise of Rene Hall (who had been left out of the production after a blow-up with Klein) to fully exploit Sam's strengths, and he was flown in to retool the arrangements. Sam, in a panic, had reverted to his soft-shoe routine, so Hall concentrated on choosing songs Sam was comfortable with singing rather than songs that made him sound forced and unnatural. The Saturday night show went much smoother as Sam's performance beamed with rejuvenated confidence. Satisfied that they were finally ready, the group packed up and left the Catskills, heading two hours southeast toward the bright lights of New York City.

It was here Sam should've taken a step back and analyzed the series of events that had just occurred. He should've questioned the reason why Rene Hall hadn't been there in the first place. Here was Sam, approaching the biggest show of his life without the man who knew his limitations better than anyone. Remember, it was Hall that arranged his million-selling singles "You Send Me" and "I'll Come Running Back to You" at Specialty. It was Sam's reunion with Hall at RCA that helped him blast to the top of the Pop and R&B charts in 1962. Sam should've realized that he needed

Rene Hall to be there in the trenches with him if nobody else. But instead, Sam muddled through a poorly-arranged first show in upstate New York while Hall sat idly by in Los Angeles.

Divide and conquer is a tactic that dates back circa 500 B.C. to Sun Tzu's military treatise *The Art of War*. Sam was slowly being separated from the business associates closest to him, first with the firing of his good friend Johnnie Morisette, then Zelda Sands and Rene Hall. It was the same approach that would befall the Beatles years later. Within weeks of having secured three of the four Beatles under management in 1969, Allen Klein fired 16 of their closest associates. Everyone from the Head of Apple Records to the office secretary either had their work taken away or was left to feel so uncomfortable at the workplace, they were forced to quit. Beatles General Manager Alistair Taylor's alienation was so swift and deep, he claimed he couldn't even reach the group members by telephone. Taylor would go twenty years before talking to Paul McCartney again.

Sam was generally one to put his foot down, but at this particular time he was too focused on exorcising his Copa demons to see what was going on around him. He normally would have demanded Rene Hall be included in his show, and that any disagreements between Hall and Klein be put to the side at least for the Copa run. But Hall was on board now, the arrangements went over great, and all was right with the world in Sam's eyes—he was armed and ready to take on the Copacabana.

> *Once a task has begun,*
> *Never leave it 'til it's done.*
> *Be the task great or small,*
> *Do it well or not at all.*

Backstage at the Copa, Sam Cooke paced the floor with nervous anticipation. He had flown Dot Holloway in from D.C. to be by his side opening night. "He was nervous, but excited," she recalled. "There were a lot of people coming backstage to say 'hello' and to wish him good luck, and to let him know they were there for support." According to Charles, it was pouring down rain outside, but it didn't deter the long line of people waiting to get in the club. He also remembered how Klein ticked Sam off as he was getting dressed earlier in the evening:

"He didn't take no shit from Klein. (He) would throw him out of the room in a minute. Klein wanted to make Sam put on a sport coat for the show. Sam said 'man, I've got on a $500 shirt. Why would I…Charlie, put that fucker outta here!' I said, (fighting laughter) 'C'mon, man, you gotta go!'"

Sam understood the magnitude of his return to the Copacabana and the last thing he needed was unnecessary stress. Tonight was, in essence, the ultimate test of his resolve as an entertainer, as well as the make-or-break opportunity that could determine the direction of his career. As if the pressure for Sam to succeed wasn't great enough, more than a week before Sam's opening night Allen Klein commissioned a giant illuminated billboard that read "Who's the Biggest Cook in Town?" in the middle of Times Square. As the day of his arrival got closer, the billboard was changed to reveal the answer: "Sam's the Biggest Cooke in Town," complete with his picture with outstretched arms. Sam knew that failure here would severely cripple his high-end marketability, and that his cycle of national tours and featured one-nighters would more than likely continue for the next several years. By the same token, a successful Copa run could open doors to more lucrative and classier sets, and maybe even give Sam the chance to star on Broadway or the silver screen. For all of the work he had put in over the years, the direction of his career came down to these next few performances.

The show opened with an introduction from Sammy Davis, Jr. It contained the typical warm-hearted accolades except for one small nuance. "It was a recording," Charles recalls. "Sammy Davis had just left there. He made a recording introducing Sam." The band's initial punch on the intro of "The Best Things in Life are Free" served to establish the energy level Sam expected from the mostly white, conservative audience. "There were just a few of 'us' in the crowd," Dot noted. The song is most synonymous with Frank Sinatra, yet Sam is careful not to clean it up as much as he would have in his first go-round at the Copa. He does sing the first verse with textbook diction, but by the second time around, he relaxes—the sunbeams that shine are "yoze and they mine y'all." Sam realized there is a way to sing to this crowd, and it involved getting the ethnic balance just right. He now understood that with that perfect balance he could win this crowd over, enjoy himself, and still maintain his dignity by the time the curtain closed.

The rest of the songs that night played out in much the same fashion, with Sam shifting his focus on "entertaining the crowd" as opposed to "gettin' down," and he purposely refrained from breaking into his signature gospel rifts. Between songs, he was as precise with his choice of words as he was the songs themselves, and as a result sounded more deliberate than he would in everyday speech. By the time he segued into song however, his performance was convincing enough that his refined dialogue went unnoticed. Sam already had the uncanny ability to captivate both gospel and pop audiences. If his performance this night was any indication of the way he'd approach supper-club sophisticates going forward, then Sam was on his way to striking gold once again.

Enough credit can't be given to those behind him. Rene Hall's arrangements, once again, complemented Sam perfectly. Even if Sam botched a verse like he did in "If I Had a Hammer," he was comfortable enough with the song to find his way back on track. His supper-club band (he had a different band for pop venues), which included Albert "June" Gardner on drums and Clif White on guitar, were all hand-picked and some of the best in the business. Given time, Sam and his entourage would have figured out that call-and-response numbers were not as popular in supper clubs, and Sam would have undoubtedly written new material with this venue in mind. He did sing the pop-driven "You Send Me" in a medley and the rock and roll song "Twistin' the Night Away" in its entirety, but over the course of time he would have introduced the sophisticates to more R&B-laden and gospel-driven works, once again shedding his crossover skin for the true Sam Cooke.

Sam did find a way to work political messages into his performance that opening night. While a song like "A Change is Gonna Come" would have been far too radical, the interactive "If I Had a Hammer" carried a theme of racial unity, and Sam sang "Blowin' in the Wind" in a sing-song fashion that didn't allow the audience to dwell on the social impact of Dylan's lyrics. Sam's return to the Copa was a series of get-me-over performances, and while he expected the act to appear polished from the opening night, he wouldn't be completely satisfied with it until he had a few runs like this one under his belt. With continued tweaking of the play list and more comfortable dialogue, Sam would undoubtedly have this audience right where he had all of his others—in his back pocket.

Regardless of any minor faults, Sam's run at the Copa was a resounding success. The club patrons responded to his performances with thunderous applause. Newspapers and magazines who knew him mostly from his pop material, praised the strength of his diverse talent (if they had only known what he did to gospel crowds!). Sam had passed the test. He now had closure on the one performance that had haunted him his entire pop career. "Sam was proud of himself," Dot noted. The great task Sam had begun was now done, and he had done it well.

Opening night, Allen Klein called Sam outside because there was someone he wanted him to meet. Sam, aware that it was still raining heavily, told Klein to call the person inside, but Klein insisted Sam come out. As the hotel's double doors swung open, a photographer captured the now-famous picture of Sam's surprise as Klein and J.W. Alexander greeted Sam with a brand new Rolls-Royce, complete with a ribbon and bow.

In the 2003 ABKCO release of the "Sam Cooke at the Copa" Super Audio CD, Peter Guralnick's liner notes contain an interesting but inaccurate account of this picture (oddly enough, the same picture appears in Guralnick's liner notes from the 1994 ABKCO CD "Sam Cooke's SAR Records Story," with Alexander mysteriously airbrushed out). The picture is deceiving because it was shot at the precise moment Sam was caught by surprise, but truth be told, Sam wasn't that impressed by the car at all.

For starters, the picture was taken *after* the opening night's show, not before. Secondly, Sam may have commented on the beauty of the car at one time, but a Rolls-Royce wasn't his cup of tea, and he really had no interest in owning one. Its true Sam loved foreign cars, but he preferred the sound and speed of a good sports car, not a touring car like a Rolls-Royce. Sam loved the rush of the wind a good convertible provided, and he wasn't too shy to test the limits of his Jaguar or Ferrari, top down, on the freeways of Southern California. While he did seem shocked in the picture, the car wasn't even important enough to Sam to risk getting wet in order to give it a close inspection. In fact, after seeing it, his reaction was "that's nice." He then turned around and went back into the hotel. Sam shipped the car back to California, but only drove it once or twice a month.

It wasn't that Sam was still upset about the sport coat fiasco. Sam was the type of person who didn't hold a grudge over matters so small; he could blow up one minute and forget it the next. What was interesting is that Sam's attitude towards the car reflected what he was starting to feel about Allen Klein. Klein's time as Sam's manager was nearing an end, and a luxury car couldn't prolong the inevitable. Klein had gotten Sam the back royalties and new contract from RCA, and he had upheld his promise of getting Sam another run at the Copa. But Sam was starting to mistrust Klein and though he had no definitive proof, the gnawing feeling in his gut was telling him something wasn't right. I asked Dot, who Sam trusted and talked with intimately, did Sam think Allen Klein was shady. Her answer, almost before I could complete the question, was a resounding "Yep."

With both sides of his latest release "Good Times"/Tennessee Waltz" climbing up the charts, the annual Cook family reunion in the summer of 1964 should've been his chance to relax and reflect on his recent accomplishments, but that simply wasn't the case. If anything, Sam's return to Chicago revealed the fact that he was indeed a troubled man.

"Sam had this thing he would do, this mannerism when he was stressed or in deep thought," Gene recalls. He spoke as if he still felt Sam's level of concern. "He would take his index finger and his thumb and hold them between his eyes with his eyes closed. I remember him walking away from the rest of the family and into a bedroom at my grandmother's house and sitting there like that. He sat there for a long, long time, not moving. He looked sad. That's when I realized for the first time something was wrong."

Sam was always the life of the party but this summer he was wound too tightly to even enjoy the family picnic. Sam had spent the last six months focusing on the Copa and it seemed that after the excitement died down, he realized he may have gotten in too deep with Allen Klein. Gene distinctly remembered an odd conversation Sam had with Papa:

"I remember when I first heard Sam or anyone else for that matter, talk back to Papa. They were in dialogue; they weren't shouting, weren't screaming, but I heard Sam tell Papa he didn't know what he was talking about. He said 'You don't understand, Papa. I live in a different world. The world I live in is a dog-eat-dog world, and I have to eat them before they eat me.' We were at the family picnic and Sam and Papa argued all the way back to the limo. Me and Maurice got into the limo with them. We were playing in the back of the limo, or at least acting like we were playing, then we started listening. We heard Sam tell Papa he didn't need Klein any more after his new record deal and his run at the Copa. Papa said 'What? I didn't raise you to use people! I raised you to be a Christian!' Sam said 'Christian? I'm talking about the record business, Papa, the entertainment business. It's a cutthroat, dirty world I live in. You just <u>don't</u> understand!'"

Besides his problems with Klein, Sam had to deal with some uninvited visitors during his run at the Copa. He was used to brushes with underworld characters in L.A., but the visit in New York rattled Sam—the severity of his situation had now extended beyond the west coast. Because the heat had intensified, the pressure he was under started to take its toll. Sam began to drink more and his face was puffier as a result. Small bags were starting to form under his eyes and his jovial nature nearly eroded due to constant stress. Sam began to adopt a more serious outlook on life. He became driven by a determination to dig even deeper into the trenches in order to avoid relinquishing his whole life's work.

The pressures Sam faced were not unique; in fact they were quite common. Elvis Presley, in an interview with Larry Geller, gave his synopsis of what went on behind closed doors:

Larry, this is a dangerous universe. It's dangerous. No matter who you are, the higher you are, the more dangerous it is. In the twenties and the thirties the gangs would mow you down in the streets, or they'd dump your body in the river. Now those people are legitimate in business. They're businessmen, they run corporations.

The saving grace for Elvis may have been his worldwide popularity. It was thought that the spotlight on Elvis was too big to arouse negative attention, and that "the gangs" didn't push for control of his career for that reason. Unfortunately, Sam Cooke didn't share that same luxury.

Sam realized he had painted himself into a corner. In a perfect world, his success at the Copa would've served as his springboard to classier venues. In reality, Sam had to face the fact that unscrupulous forces were prevalent in the recording and entertainment industries and that he would be blackballed from sophisticated supper clubs unless he went along with the program. Las Vegas, for the same reason, was definitely out of the question. Sam's success at the Copa in the summer of 1964 should've opened new doors to his career, but instead it opened a can of worms Sam wasn't prepared to deal with.

Chapter Twelve

Sam's Final Hours

SAM'S HEADACHE WAS ACCOMPANIED BY a now-too-familiar dizziness as he made his way out of bed and into the den, bracing himself on the couch's arm as he slowly lowered his body onto the cushion. He took a deep breath, propped a pillow behind his head and closed his watered eyes until the throbbing pain subsided. The date was December 9, 1964, and the man who invented Soul was wrestling the grip of influenza. Once Sam regained his equilibrium, he steadied his focus on the telephone's rotary face and began to dial the number. He smiled with the realization that no matter how bad he felt, he had to call his youngest sister Agnes to wish her a happy 29th birthday.

Gene was the one that answered the phone that day. "We talked for a while before he said 'Let me speak to *Snags*.' That's how we always knew it was him calling; he would always ask to speak to *Snags*. Sam called my mother that ever since she lost her two front teeth as a little girl."

"It was just a general brother-to-sister conversation," Agnes recalls. "He told me he had the flu, and he hadn't been out of the house in almost a week. We talked about the weather here because it was so cold, and he teased me about how warm the weather was in California. He told me he had mailed Christmas presents to me, Mary, Hattie, and my mother and to look out for them. We talked almost an hour about the weather, about family and about stuff that was happening here. He rarely talked business, or at least to me anyway. He did say that if he felt better, he was going to try to make it into the office tomorrow (Thursday, the 10th)."

Sam lived life to the fullest, and quite often burned the candle at both ends. He was an entertainer, business owner, husband, father, brother and son. When he was in Los Angeles he could be found anywhere from his SAR Records office, to his guest house that doubled as an at-home studio, to RCA's Hollywood studios, to the Soul Workshop in South

Central Inglewood. Sam's days were spent writing, recording and producing not just for himself, but for artists on the two record labels he ran as well. Once the sun set, he often frequented L.A.'s nightclubs until the wee hours of the morning. All of this of course, was predicated on him even being in Los Angeles. He still went out on headline engagements from time to time, and often visited his family in Chicago or RCA's headquarters in New York.

Charles, Sam and friends out on the town.

(Photo courtesy of Charlene Graham)

That being said, when Sam was forced to stay at home and reflect on his life and career, major decisions would often result from his solace and meditation. Ironically, there also seemed to be something about the beginning of a new year which motivated Sam into making a fresh start. In late 1958, while emotionally recovering from a near-fatal car accident, he decided to take control of his career and formed the SAR partnership in early 1959. Later that year he decided to leave Keen Records and signed his historic deal with RCA in January of 1960. The decision to revisit the Copacabana was made as he lamented over the loss of his young son Vincent, and he began preparation for a second run at the Copa in January of 1964. And now in December, after spending a week in bed battling the flu, he came to accept the fact that major changes had to be made in 1965 for both his personal life and professional career.

From a personal standpoint, Sam was going to start the New Year off by investing in businesses for each of his brothers and sisters.

"We were at my mother's house and Sam told us whatever we wanted to do," Agnes recalls, "He was going to finance a business for us and show us how to run it. He left it up to us as individuals to choose the type of business and he was going to get us up and running. Hattie and I said we were going to go into the restaurant business."

"Mary did hair, and he was going to open up a beauty salon for her," David remembers. "Sam had always said Atlanta was an up-and-coming city for blacks and he was going to invest money there to open up a car wash for me, L.C., and Charles to own. He was going to do something for everybody in the family."

Professionally, Sam knew that the time had come to cut ties with Allen Klein. After the Copa buzz died down, Sam regretted Klein's firing of Zelda Sands who was not only a valuable and trusted employee, but a good friend as well. It wasn't until Sam was confined to bed rest, however, did he start to review the financial records of Tracey Ltd. and her subsidiaries, and he did not like what he saw. Sam had hinted to friends like Bumps Blackwell his growing mistrust in Allen Klein and Klein's involvement in his business affairs, and over the years Eddie Jamison expressed his suspicions to the family that Klein may have taken control of Sam's business entities without his knowledge. Also, costs that Sam assumed were absorbed by RCA, like the illuminated billboard for the Copa and the Rolls-Royce Sam received as a "present," had allegedly been buried as expenses in his financial statements. Once Sam had a chance to sit back and review his company's records, the magnitude of myriad irregularities came to light.

According to court records, there had been $141,329.45 in expenses charged to Sam through KAGS and Tracey, of which $7,705.24 went to Marvin Drager, Inc., the public relations firm hired by Klein to handle all Copa-related publicity. The monies paid to Drager, broken down over 15 varied payments, included the expenses for the billboard. Even earlier in the year, $1088.87 had been charged to KAGS on February 29, 1964 under the notation "RCA Victor-The Tonight Show Band," as well as $585.00 from March 2, 1964 entered as "NBC." These expenses were in connection with the extra musicians that were hired for Sam's February 7th performance of "A Change is Gonna Come" on *The Tonight Show*. In "Dream Boogie," author Guralnick stated that "(Allen Klein) would get RCA to pay for a full string section and all the extra musicians Sam needed, and if (RCA Exec) Joe D'Imperio wouldn't spring for it, Allen would pay for it out of his own pocket," and more than likely Klein gave Sam that same impression. But from the list of expenses, it was clear that neither Klein nor RCA footed the bill for the extra musicians—KAGS did. That gnawing feeling in Sam's gut was now telling him changes had to be made—and made in a hurry.

By the end of 1964, Sam had already made up his mind to divorce Barbara. Since Vincent's death in the summer of 1963 the couple's relationship hadn't been the same. It was no secret she dated outside the marriage, and Sam had never relinquished his love for Dot Holloway:

"We were supposed to meet in Puerto Rico when baby Vincent drowned. Sam called me and told me the baby had drowned and he had to cancel the whole trip. Sam believed it was because Barbara was not paying enough attention to the kids. But we were together the month before he died, and we were seriously talking about getting back together. My divorce was final, I was free at the time, and Sam was talking about leaving Barbara. He believed if she had not been doing what she was doing and running with that Bobby Womack guy, things may have been different, but he had made up his mind he was going to finally leave her."

My aunts and uncles confirm Sam's plans to leave Barbara, and it's quite possible she suspected the same thing. Phyllis and Charles remembered being confused about receiving their Christmas gifts in late October and wondered why Barbara mailed them so early, but in retrospect they realized it was probably because she had seen the writing on the wall. More than likely, the marriage wouldn't have lasted that far into the New Year.

Sam regained partial strength on Thursday, the 10th, and felt well enough to go into the office. Over the past several months Sam noticed how he and his old gospel partner J.W. Alexander were growing distant, and that J.W. was more and more at Klein's beck and call. Alexander's persistence on arranging a meeting with Klein, then his insistence Sam retain Klein's managerial services concerned Sam, but what he found amongst Tracey's *List of Officers, Directors and Agent* was more than enough to seal Alexander's fate from both a personal and professional standpoint: J.W. had registered Tracey Limited with Allen Klein as Tracey's Secretary, Director, and sole owner.

Taking a chronological look at Tracey Limited's corporate structure from its inception, it isn't difficult to see that the drastic changes that took place in the company were probably not to Sam's knowledge and certainly not to his advantage. The *Articles of Incorporation of Tracey Limited*, signed before a notary public in September of 1963 by Sam Cooke, James W. Alexander, and S.R. Crain, seem to be in ordinary order. However, the alleged events leading up to Tracey's incorporation, and the subsequent Tracey-related listings filed in the State of Nevada are disturbing to say the least.

Sam was headlining a tour with an all-star cast that included Dion, Bobby "Blue" Bland, and Little Willie John when, according to Peter Guralnick's "Dream Boogie," Allen Klein met Sam after his September 26th show in New Orleans. It was on this Thursday night Sam and Klein supposedly shared a "tender moment" as Klein delivered a six-figure check for past-due royalties from RCA and Sam subsequently asked Klein to be his manager. Klein then stated "I had to get a flight back to New York early the next morning" because of the Yom Kippur holiday which started that Friday, September 27th.

IN WITNESS WHEREOF, we have hereunto subscribed our names, this *27* day of *Sept* , 1963.

_____
Sam Cooke

_____
James Alexander

_____
S. R. Crain

STATE OF *New York,*
COUNTY OF *New York,* SS.:

On this *27* day of *Sept* , 1963, personally appeared before me, a Notary Public in and for the state and county aforesaid, SAM COOKE, JAMES ALEXANDER, and S. R. CRAIN, known to me to be the persons described in and who executed the foregoing instrument who acknowledged to me that they executed the same freely and voluntarily and for the uses and purposes therein mentioned.

WITNESS my hand and official seal, the day and year in these Articles first above written.

_____
Notary Public
ADRIENNE THERESA ZANGHI (GOLDFARB)
Notary Public, State of New York
No. 03-9787608
Qualified in Bronx County
Commission Expires March 30, 1964

Tracey Limited's Articles of Incorporation *signature page, as signed September 27, 1963.*

What was interesting was that neither Klein nor Guralnick ever mentioned Sam and his business associates being in New York on Friday, September 27ᵗh—after Sam's New Orleans show but before his October 4ᵗh engagement in Columbus, Ohio. In Tracey's *Articles of Incorporation*, Notary Public Adrienne Zanghi Goldfarb attests to the fact that Sam Cooke, S.R. Crain and J.W. Alexander *personally appeared before her* in the state of New York on September 27, 1963. If Klein knew that Sam and his associates were to be in New York to sign legal documents on Friday the 27ᵗh, why would he go to New Orleans the night before?

The thought of Allen Klein delivering Sam's check in person doesn't add up for several reasons. First and foremost, Allen Klein did not represent Sam Cooke in any official capacity—he simply performed an accounting audit on Sam's behalf. Why would Klein have the RCA check, valued at approximately $120,000, in his possession in the first place? According to Guralnick, Sam didn't even *ask* for Klein's representation until they talked in New Orleans. It doesn't make sense that RCA would release a six-figure check to a non-entity instead of giving it directly to their employee, Sam Cooke, who was scheduled to be in town the very next day. And what could Sam, a black man traveling in the South in 1963, possibly do with an out-of-state check that size anyway?

Also worth noting, Yom Kippur is Judaism's most important holiday, a day of total Sabbath. During the Sabbath, orthodox Jews are forbidden from functions others take for granted in everyday life—eating, drinking (even water), and operating machinery (including driving a car, watching television, or flipping on a light switch). The 25-hour fasting period starts the sunset before Yom Kippur (the evening of the 26th in this case) and ends the nightfall of the day itself. While there are exceptions to the rules and while each person adopts their own set of standards, activities like flying in an airplane and conducting business transactions during Yom Kippur tend to go against traditional interpretations.

As if accepting the general premise of events wasn't difficult enough, I was even more skeptical of the scenario Guralnick painted of Sam Cooke urging a reluctant Allen Klein to become his manager. The conversation, which supposedly took place in the bedroom of the New Orleans hotel room, sounded more like a teenage love story than a business transaction. According to Guralnick, Klein was initially awkward about asking Sam for his finder's fee from the RCA negotiation, until Sam took control of the situation and wrote him a check. Then, after Klein shied away from the idea of being Sam's manager, Sam assured him it was only natural to be nervous about trying something new. This "released a flood of emotion" in Klein because Sam "put his finger on Allen's vulnerability" and his "need to be loved." I don't know Allen Klein personally, but I have a feeling he didn't need his confidence boosted by Sam Cooke or anyone else in order to accept a commission check or managerial job. And for the record, it was Allen Klein who aggressively sought to represent Sam Cooke, not the other way around.

In this same bedroom meeting with Sam in New Orleans, Klein notes that his attorney, Martin Machat, was standing on the hotel balcony overlooking Bourbon Street and not in the same room with the two of them. Why would Klein bother bringing his attorney with him if he were just in town to deliver a check? Klein admitted they didn't get a chance to see Sam's show that night, which was strange in itself. And according to Klein, Sam initiated the representation discussion there in the hotel room, so Machat didn't come to New Orleans with those negotiations in mind. Once Sam and Klein did start talking about a business deal, you would think that Klein would've attempted to have a legal document, no matter how rudimentary, prepared by Machat and signed on the spot. But according to Klein, Machat was on the balcony admiring the majestic Big Easy, never participating in the non-contractual, verbal agreement his client was entering into in the next room.

Klein went on to say how he was happy to receive a "finder's fee" from Sam for services rendered because he desperately needed the money to pay bills. If he were so strapped for cash, why would he make a useless trip to New Orleans and pay the airfare and hotel costs for not just himself, but his lawyer as well? Surely Machat was being paid for his time, and because his services weren't utilized, what was his purpose for being there?

We can't ignore the documented fact that Sam Cooke, S. R. Crain, and J.W. Alexander were in New York signing the *Articles of Incorporation* for Tracey on September 27, 1963. So why would Klein bother revealing the details of this heart-wrenching New Orleans hotel visit on the 26ᵗʰ, a visit which made no sense, I personally don't believe occurred, and is almost impossible to verify? Because on the surface, this feel-good story serves to paint the picture of a warm friendship and intimate bond between Sam Cooke and Allen Klein, a bond which never really existed on a personal or professional level. Deep down, Sam never really trusted Klein, which may be why their business relationship was never sealed with a contract. In reality, their head-strong, take-charge personalities probably caused more conflict than harmony.

Sam's intuition was on point, because behind the scenes there were some questionable moves made by Klein and Alexander. Since my original search in 2004, I've managed to locate the *List of Officers, Directors and Agent* as recorded in the State of Nevada for the years Tracey Limited was a corporation. For the period of July 1, 1963 to July 1, 1964, the documents filed by J.W. Alexander on October 14, 1963 list Sam Cooke as President, Alexander as Vice-President, and Allen Klein as Secretary. The Directors of the company are Sam, J.W., and Klein respectively. Curiously enough, the address listed for all three officers is Allen Klein's New York City business address, despite the fact that Sam and J.W. operated out of Los Angeles. Unlike Tracey's *Articles of Incorporation*, there is no mention of Papa Cook serving on the Board of Directors in the *List of Officers* J.W. Alexander officially filed.

Tracey Limited's List of Officers, Directors, and Agent *for 1963-1964 as filed in Nevada on October 14, 1963 by J.W. Alexander.*

Tracey Limited's List of Officers, Directors, and Agent *for 1964-1965 as filed in Nevada on April 27, 1964 by Allen Klein.*

Sam Cooke, still on tour in October of 1963, was more than likely unaware of these developments.

If this *List of Officers* filing didn't cause Sam to sit up from his sickbed, the next one certainly did. The List for the period of July 1, 1964 to July 1, 1965, filed by Allen Klein himself on April 27, 1964, had J.W. Alexander as the President of Tracey Limited and Allen Klein as Secretary *and* Treasurer. Sam had been given a title—Chairman of the Board—but his name was categorized under the heading OFFICERS WHO ARE NOT DIRECTORS. Simply put, Sam Cooke had no power or control in his "own" company. Stunned and betrayed, Sam met with his ex-agent Jess Rand in Los Angeles on the afternoon of December 10th and said "Get me the best Jewish lawyer in New York! Fuck it. Get me *two* of the best Jewish lawyers in New York! I'll be there first thing Monday morning!"

Unfortunately, this wasn't the first time Sam had his suspicions about J.W. Zelda remembered an incident at SAR's office several months earlier that seemed to upset Sam:

"One time Sam was going down a list that I had made of all the songs and writers in the whole (KAGS) catalog. On one of the songs he says 'what's J.W.'s name doing on this one? He didn't...' and he started to say something and he stopped. I knew something was very wrong. It was one of the really early records Sam wrote, before I had started working there. He was very disturbed over that."

One of Sam's pet peeves was that he hated liars with a passion. As generous as Sam was as a person, once you lied to him there was no second chance. If he caught you in a lie he wasn't the type to say "the next time you do it, that's it," nor would he shout, scream or make a scene. He was known to hit you a look of disgust, then turn his back to you and walk away. It was commonly thought that the finality of Sam's cold shoulder was much harder to accept than his temporary bursts of heated wrath. Sam was now convinced his manager Allen Klein had been manipulating his business affairs, and it also seemed his business partner and long-time friend J.W. Alexander had been in on the conspiracy. He also felt that Barbara had not only let her social habits get out of control, but covered it up to the point it cost Sam his youngest son's life. To Sam, three people in his circle were liars, and for that reason they would all have to be purged from his life for 1965. In one swift visit to New York Sam planned to dissolve all ties between him, Allen Klein and J.W. Alexander, then return to Los Angeles to start divorce proceedings against Barbara.

Because of their deceit, Sam's separation from the three of them would have been an easy one as far as he was concerned. No one in the family knows if Sam called Allen Klein in New York and told him ahead of time about his plans to relieve him of his accounting and managerial duties, but it was well known amongst family members that Sam had decided to drop Klein and buy out Alexander in order to begin 1965 with a clean slate. He would focus on securing his family members financially and recruiting talent for his record labels (perhaps he came to accept the fact that he'd probably be blackballed from the supper-club circuit). Removing Klein, Alexander, and Barbara would have required a level of realignment in his life, but the lightened burden and fresh start would be a fair exchange for any old partnerships and memories shared between them.

At the other end of the spectrum, things weren't so cut and dried. While Sam wouldn't have had a problem coping with the changes, a great deal of Klein, Alexander and Barbara Cooke's livelihood depended on Sam. It would have been a devastating blow to them financially for Sam to walk out the door. Klein, at the time, had not yet broken through with the Beatles or Rolling Stones. Sam Cooke was his hottest act by far, and it didn't help his case that the two had never signed a formal agreement. If Sam were somehow able to wrest control of SAR Records, KAGS Music Publishing, and the parent company Tracey Limited by proving criminal intent, then Klein and J.W. Alexander would've not only been crippled financially, they probably would've ended up in prison.

For Barbara, Sam's divorce would mean an end to the extravagant lifestyle she had become accustomed to as the pampered wife of a famous celebrity. Even more important to her at the time was her steady access to cash. Sam had initially been sympathetic to a financial bind she had gotten herself into and paid off her "line of credit." But after Vincent's death

Sam refused to pay her debts, and Barbara knew that once he walked, she would be left alone to deal with them herself. Besides that, what would she do? Go back to Chicago, look for a job, and live in shame as she tried to explain her fall from grace? Once Sam cut the purse strings, the future would be anything but rosy for the three individuals in question.

The events that took place after Sam's meeting with Jess Rand have always left me puzzled. According to Daniel Wolff's biography "You Send Me," Sam went to Rand's office without much cash in his pocket. After their meeting, it was said that he withdrew $5,000 from a safe deposit box in the building's Union Savings Bank, possibly to complete some Christmas shopping. While this may not have been an unusual transaction, it was a private transaction, and I always wondered how Rand could be sure Sam withdrew $5 or $5000 from his personal box, especially *after* he had left his office.

What's even more confusing is that in E! Entertainment's 1999 episode of "Mysteries & Scandals", Jess Rand said that Sam told him he wanted to get a lot of his Christmas shopping done because he was going to be on the road. Though Rand never said it directly, the show alleged that Rand cashed one of Sam's personal checks for this purpose, even going so far as to dramatize a black man's hand writing out a check in Jess Rand's name. Are we to assume Rand had $5000 in cash (enough to buy a new 1964 Chevy Corvette) lying around his office in exchange for Sam's check?

The idea of Sam going Christmas shopping seems highly unlikely, though it's a constant in both stories. From Agnes' conversation with Sam on her birthday, he told her he had already sent Christmas presents back home to his family in Chicago. "I remember it was real eerie," Agnes recalls, "because we all received our gifts on the 11th, the same day Sam died." If he had additional presents to buy, Sam carried several major credit cards and would not have to withdraw such a large sum of cash to do so. It wouldn't make sense for him to shower Barbara with expensive gifts right before he slapped her with divorce papers, and if he planned to buy a discreet present, he certainly wouldn't worry about explaining a credit card bill to a "lame duck" wife.

Those who knew Sam knew it was not out of the ordinary for him to carry large sums of money. He often kept several hundred dollars on his person and on occasion he'd hold onto large-denomination bills ($500, $1000, even $5000) as a novelty. If Sam made a transaction that day, I highly doubt it was $5000 for Christmas presents. However, if one didn't know he had already completed his Christmas shopping, this would seem like a reasonable explanation for why he was carrying that much money. I believe that emphasizing Sam's withdrawal earlier in the day helped validate the events that would occur over the next several hours. Why else would it be so important to note that Sam had at least $5000 on his person, important to the point that stories conflict as to the money's origin?

If you sense skepticism on my part, you are correct. There are many inconsistencies about what happened in Sam's last hours; some dealing with vastly conflicting stories, others with Sam drastically departing from what the family knew to be his normal activities. Most people tend to be creatures of habit, and Sam was no different. On the road, S.R. Crain carried Sam's "money" briefcase containing fifteen thousand dollars or more in live-show proceeds because he didn't trust leaving the money in a hotel or in his private limo. In the city, however, Sam didn't make a habit of carrying an amount like five thousand dollars. In addition, there was no evidence he ever went shopping or bought anything of significant value that day.

Assuming Sam had a large amount of cash on him for whatever reason, he felt well enough that evening to go to Martoni's, an Italian restaurant frequented by Hollywood actors, singers, agents, and wannabes. Zelda Sands insisted that if Sam wanted to break into more sophisticated venues, Martoni's was the kind of place he could network, and Sam took her advice and made the restaurant one of his regular hangouts. From the best re-creation of events that night, Sam had a dinner date with record producer Al Schmitt and his wife Joan and arrived at the restaurant around 9:00 p.m. They ordered martinis at the bar until their table was ready.

While the three were seated at the bar, a record label public relations man walked in with his 22-year-old Asian escort, Lisa Boyer. Sam acknowledged them both and they made small talk until their table was ready. Before taking their table, Sam pulled out what Joan Schmitt described as "several thousand dollars" to pay the bar tab, piquing the interest of Boyer and other patrons. Sam and the Schmitts had appetizers and ordered dinner, but before the main entrée was served, Sam excused himself and stayed absent for several minutes. Al Schmitt went to look for Sam and found him at the bar talking to Lisa Boyer. Sam never returned for dinner, but promised to meet Al at a club called PJ's on Sunset Boulevard at around 1:00 a.m. The Schmitts left Martoni's at around 10:45 p.m. while the patrons at the bar say that Sam left with Lisa between 12:30 a.m. and 1:30 a.m.

In that short passage of time, I found one thing strikingly odd: what was this public relations guy doing while Sam spent hours at the bar talking to Lisa? Isn't it strange that Lisa spent most of her "date" talking to and then leaving with Sam? Could that have been the plan?

The rest of the story is continued from testimony at the Los Angeles County coroner's inquest, an inquest whose shoddy investigation was curious from the very beginning. When Lisa Boyer was asked by the L.A. County coroner when was the first time she met Sam Cooke in her life, she replied "well, we spoke to each other on Thursday evening," not making it clear whether she met Sam that night or not. Her answer was never challenged. She then went on to say they were "at a dinner party in Hollywood," where he "got up and sang." Martoni's was a public restaurant, they never dined together, and no one else remembered Sam getting up to sing. In fact, the restaurant didn't have a stage or a microphone. Again, these statements were never challenged at the inquest.

According to Boyer's testimony, Sam and Lisa left Martoni's and arrived at PJ's at 1:40 a.m., about 20 minutes before closing time. Sam talked with a couple of friends, but almost got into a tussle with a man that tried to talk to Lisa at the bar. Since PJ's was closing anyway, they decided to leave, and an emotionally-shaken Lisa asked to be taken home. But instead of making the proper turn, Sam jumped on the Hollywood Freeway, heading back towards downtown, telling her they were just "going for a ride." She says Sam ignored her persistent pleas to be taken home by telling her she was "just a lovely girl, and how he just thought he was madly in love" with her. Disregarding her desire to go home, at 2:35 a.m. Sam pulled his red 1965 Ferrari into the Hacienda Motel in Watts, a $3 per night establishment widely regarded as a hooker's motel.

It doesn't take a conspiracy theorist to admit the story to this point seems a little strange. Here is a man with a reported $5000 in his pocket, driving miles out of his way to go to a $3 motel in one of the most dangerous parts of town with a woman who didn't want to go there in the first place. Disregard the cleanliness factor of a motel like the Hacienda. Disregard the fact that Sam's exotic new convertible (the *next* model year's Ferrari) was found top down and running in one of the poorest, highest-crime areas of Los Angeles. Even disregard the fact that he passed dozens of quality hotels on the way to this particular dump. Once the Cook family heard that Sam forcibly took a woman to a sleazy motel, the story immediately lost all credibility. Sam routinely turned away scores of sexual advances, so for him to take any woman anywhere against her will was absurd to those who knew Sam best. David remembered one of his initial reactions being "Sam wouldn't let *me* stay at a $3 motel, let alone check himself into one!" Also, cheesy tactics like telling a woman how he was "madly in love" with her did not fit Sam's character.

Continuing with Lisa Boyer's testimony, Sam pulled into the motel parking lot, walked into the manager's office and proceeded to pay for a room. While it would've made sense for someone held against their will to use this as an opportunity for escape (she would later describe herself as a kidnap victim), Lisa Boyer instead followed Sam into the office and, in her words, said very loudly "Mr. Cooke, please take me home!" The motel manager is 55-year-old Bertha Franklin and when it's her turn to testify at the coroner's inquest she claims Lisa "didn't say anything; she didn't say a word." At any rate, Franklin noticed Lisa behind Sam and insisted he change his registration to "Mr. and Mrs." where he had previously signed his name only: Sam Cooke. It's ironic that a sleazy motel like the Hacienda had the nerve to be a stickler for certain details of moral decency.

Boyer then testified Sam took her by the arm and dragged her into the hotel room, locking the door behind them (the coroner had to restore order as the two hundred plus people in the courtroom vehemently roared "No, no!" in protest). "Please, take me home" she continued to plead loudly, but Sam pushed her onto the bed, pinning her down in the process. He told her "we're just going to talk" and then proceeded to "pull her sweater off and rip her dress off." In the middle of being assaulted, she asked Sam "Mr. Cooke, may I go to the bathroom, please?" and he allowed her to do so. After discovering the bathroom window was painted shut, she walked back into the bedroom in her bra and slip, passing a naked Sam Cooke as he decided to use the facilities himself. Finally seeing her chance to escape, Boyer picked up her clothes, unlatched the locked door, and ran to the motel manager's office for help.

If we take just a moment to analyze these events, it's not hard to see why the story of Sam Cooke's death has been considered one of the most bizarre and implausible fabrications ever allowed to stand up in court. It was reminiscent of the Richard Pryor comedy routine in which his young son's story about a broken lamp was so animated, Pryor ended up giving the child credit for his creativity rather than punish him for breaking the lamp. The only thing more unbelievable about Lisa Boyer's schoolgirl request for a bathroom break during an alleged rape was the fact the whole thing went unquestioned at the inquest. What rapist stops cold so that his victim can use the bathroom, then takes a break himself, all the while expecting his victim to wait patiently until he's finished? How successful would a rape attempt be anyway? Sam's face was easily recognizable—"ain't a black person alive didn't know Sam." Charles would say, "If they didn't know him from Gospel, they knew him from Pop"—and supposedly he signed his correct name in the registration book. And while Sam wasn't afraid to fight any man anywhere, it was always stressed by Papa Cook that under no circumstances do you ever put your hands on a woman, and Sam never did. There were almost as many "facts" that came out of this inquest that were unbelievable to the outside world as there were contradictions to Sam's nature unbelievable to the Cook family.

According to Boyer, she knocked twice at the manager's door and when she didn't receive an answer, she went around to the back of the motel and began to dress herself, only to find she had also picked up some of Sam's clothes in the process. Spotting a phone booth nearby, she dumped his clothes and called the police to tell them she had been kidnapped. The police arrived a few minutes later.

Motel Manager Bertha Lee Franklin's testimony picked up where Lisa Boyer's left off. She claimed that after she rented the room to Sam and Lisa, she received a phone call. Franklin lived in the apartment behind the manager's office and even though it's close to 3 a.m., she's talking to the motel's owner, Evelyn Card. Franklin claims she responded to a knock on the door (apparently Lisa Boyer) only to find no one there, and then returned to her phone call. Minutes later she hears another knock, and its Sam at the door, dressed in what she could see was a sport coat and no shirt, asking "where's the girl?" In a strange turn of events that was never challenged, Franklin admits that when Sam rented the room he had on "a light shirt," that he wasn't wearing a jacket. When asked by the coroner how Sam looked when he returned she said "well, he had on a jacket then."

Sam repeatedly asks "where's the girl?" then requests permission to look around the apartment. Keep in mind, Sam was supposedly wearing only a sport coat, no pants or underwear, and one shoe. Franklin told Sam to call the police, and that they were the only ones she'd let search the apartment. Sam's response was "Damn the police," and he started knocking down the door with his shoulder. Once the door jamb gave way and Sam was inside, he searched the kitchen and bedroom, then came back into the living room and grabbed both of Franklin's arms and "started twisting them and asking where was the girl." From there they got into a "tussle," and Franklin fell to the floor, with Sam on top of her. Apparently Sam is in full control because she admitted he was "still twisting my arm and holding me down there on the floor." Sam was a 33-year-old man in relatively good shape, and Bertha Lee Franklin was a slightly overweight, 55-year-old woman, but somehow Franklin managed to kick Sam off of her. She kicked Sam so far off that he needed a running start to lunge back at her, and, according to her testimony, she was able to push him back down to the floor. That's when she ran and grabbed a .22 caliber revolver off of the TV and fired three shots. When asked her distance from Sam, she replied "he wasn't too far; he was at close range". One bullet ricocheted off of the ceiling and landed on the couch. One bullet was never found. One bullet entered Sam's chest under his left armpit, piercing his left lung, heart, and right lung, embedding itself just outside his right lung. "Lady, you shot me" were supposedly Sam Cooke's last words.

I won't waste your time or mine refuting the ridiculous scenario of a semi-naked Sam Cooke being tossed around the room by a middle-aged woman; let's focus on the gunshots instead. If she pushed Sam to the floor and stood over him, then the diagonally downward path of the fatal bullet would have actually made sense, but a bullet in the ceiling would not. She testified she was at close range, and the fatal bullet was fired from an inch and a half away according to police reports, yet she only managed to hit him once in three shots. Why couldn't the third bullet be found? If the gun had been sitting on the TV all along, why didn't Franklin grab it as soon as she realized Sam was trying to break down the door? She certainly had another opportunity to go for her gun in the several seconds that passed as Sam checked the apartment's kitchen and bedroom.

But Sam wasn't done. According to Bertha Lee Franklin, he lunged at her once more, but instead of shooting him again, she hit him over the head with a stick. "It was very flimsy...the first time I hit him, it broke." When the police arrived, they found the body perched against the broken door jamb. Sam Cooke was dead.

Conveniently, the motel's owner is still on the phone and hears all the commotion on the other end. Evelyn Card states in the inquest that she heard gunfire, and then Franklin came back to the phone and told her to hang up and call the police. When Card called the police department, however, transcripts show that she momentarily tripped over her own story. When asked by the dispatcher if Card thought Franklin shot the intruder, she responded with a confusing "I don't know. I heard gunfire, and she called me on the phone." Either she heard the gunfire while she was on the phone, she never heard the gunfire and Franklin called her after the incident took place, or she was never on the phone in the first place. Again, this inconsistency was never questioned at the inquest.

Boyer had already called the police from a pay phone nine minutes earlier, and waited for them to arrive. Around 3:15 a.m., seven minutes after Boyer's call, Officer Wallace Cook (no relation) is the first to arrive at the scene. In Cook's police report Bertha Franklin states that Sam knocked on the door asking for the girl, then went away. She also added she heard a car drive from the back of the parking lot to the front, stop, and then the pounding at the door continue; suggesting Sam started to drive off but changed his mind. These actions never came up in the coroner's inquest. Cook's report also stated that after Franklin shot Sam, she laid the gun down and picked up the stick and proceeded to hit him on the head. Why would she lay down a gun holding three fresh rounds, and pick up a stick she described herself as "flimsy?" Officer Cook also reported he didn't observe any injuries to Mrs. Franklin, but that she had "a large amount of blood on her clothing."

A smug Bertha Franklin shortly after Sam's shooting. Notice the strange blood pattern on her dress—splotches instead of a defined spray—and that her hair is relatively intact despite her all-out "tussle" with Sam. There are no visible scars on Franklin's face or arms, yet she would later win a lawsuit against Sam's estate for medical expenses incurred as a result of her injuries.

(Photo © Bettman/Corbis)

Fred L. Thomas was the detective assigned to investigate the case. At the inquest he testified that the he found a money clip containing $108 and a wrist watch on the body. Of course, there was no mention of Sam's credit cards and the $5000 that he withdrew earlier. This meant that either Sam never had the money, or despite her haste to flee her "kidnapper," Lisa Boyer took the time to rifle through Sam's pants pockets before she ditched his clothes. Det. Thomas also testified that the turquoise dress Bertha Lee Franklin was wearing at the time of the shooting had "spots which appeared to be blood" and that the tests run on the spots "indicate the substance could be blood." *Spots* which *could be* blood? This was in stark contrast to the "large amount of blood" filed in the police report. He also stated the blood type had not been determined because "the process takes long." So we have a dress that may or may not have blood on it, and the blood may or may not have been Sam Cooke's. I would imagine the next step would be to wait to see if the lab results determined the substance was in fact blood, and that it matched the blood type of the deceased. But the coroner's office already felt it had enough solid evidence in this case to label the shooting "justifiable homicide." Case closed.

Atty. Martin Machat, hired by Allen Klein to represent Barbara in the proceedings, was repeatedly denied extensive questioning of the witnesses. When he tried to question Officer Cook and Bertha Franklin, he was abruptly cut off by the coroner. When the coroner finished questioning Lisa Boyer, he excused her immediately. "May I–" was the only thing Machat could blurt out before the coroner excused her again. As an added insult, he's constantly referred to as "Mr. Macheck" throughout the court documents.

The coroner's autopsy revealed a small cut and scratch on Sam's left cheek, as well as a scratch on the right side of his forehead. It seems as if Bertha Franklin, who didn't have a scratch on her, got the best of Sam in their "tussle." He also found a 2-inch lump on the right side of Sam's scalp that bulged "perceptibly" and possibly could've rendered him unconscious. Could this have been caused by the "flimsy" stick? Probably not, especially since the coroner testified there was no evidence of blood on the stick. So what we know is that Sam was hit on the head with a solid object and shot through the lungs and heart with a .22 caliber pistol. It seems that all other elements—cash withdrawals, kidnappings, rapes, robberies, broken doors, bloody dresses, flimsy sticks and flimsier testimonies—in the end prove to be illogical detours to solving a mystery built on irrational premises.

Since forensic technology has advanced tremendously since 1964, the possibility of bringing closure to a case like this seems promising. That is, until you realize that every aspect of Sam's death mysteriously doesn't exist any more. For example, it is now impossible to review the case file containing original police reports. It's been lost. Missing from police evidence is Bertha Franklin's bloodied dress, the fatal bullet, Sam's clothes, Bertha's gun, even the flimsy stick. The motel registration card Sam signed was checked by a handwriting analysis expert whose conclusion was that he "could not say definitely that this was Mr. Cooke." But it doesn't matter now, for the card, too, is missing. Also missing are pictures from the death scene. Those who have seen the originals say they portrayed a rather gruesome setting, with blood-splattered walls and Sam's naked body leaning against the broken door. The pictures have been posted in an English tabloid, but there's no way to tell if they've been retouched.

Of the missing "official" crime scene photos in Sam's case, there's one picture that seems to resurface more than the others. It shows Sam's lifeless body slumped against the broken door jamb. He's wearing the black sport coat and has one leg folded under his body. There is no visible amount of blood. Sam is naked from the waist down, though the picture I've seen is cropped where his genitals begin. I always thought of this as being an odd body position for a fighter like Sam—to look as if he's resting comfortably instead of as if he went out like a warrior. It was almost as if the body had been propped up to highlight the embarrassment of his nakedness and the humiliation of wearing one shoe.

I think it's apparent that the facts of the case more than likely aren't facts at all, so let's step back for a minute and look at the whole forest instead of the individual trees. The coroner's inquest was a joke, to say the least. The lawyer representing the widow was never given a chance to question the main witness, and Bertha Lee Franklin changed her original story several times yet avoided perjury charges. Lisa Boyer was a prostitute with an extensive record, a fact that was never allowed to be brought out in questioning. Martin Machat asked the coroner "Did you trace the occupation of the girl, Lisa Boyer?" to which the coroner's reply was "We are not concerned with the occupation of Miss Boyer." Bertha Franklin admitted she had a gun permit, but the coroner conveniently ignored the fact that she registered a .32 caliber gun, not the .22 that killed Sam Cooke. The whole inquest, including the jury's deliberations, lasted just two hours. Whoever had Sam Cooke killed took great pains to make sure it was an open and shut case.

For arguments sake, let's assume Sam Cooke never drove Lisa Boyer to the Hacienda in the first place. How, then, would one explain the various testimonies, the broken-down door, the blood on Bertha Franklin's dress, etc.? My answer: who cares? For years, people have followed paths in this case that defy logic and thus lead nowhere. The entity that had power enough to influence an inquest and see to it key evidence is "misplaced" could certainly procure a murder scene and witness testimonies. Truth be told, after Sam left PJ's, the last "public" place he was seen alive by several witnesses, the story is in the hands of some rather questionable people. Prostitute Lisa Boyer, Motel Manager (and ex-prostitute herself) Bertha Franklin, and Evelyn Card (whose phone records were never checked), were the characters whose testimony the inquest took for gospel. The inquest did provide an eyewitness: motel patron Alexander Prado claimed he saw Lisa offer Sam a small amount of resistance in the parking lot, but that she wasn't forcefully dragged into the hotel room. He also stated he didn't hear any gun shots because he went back to bed. Prado's useless testimony did nothing but cloud an already ambiguous case.

The story that's been kicked around for years was that Bertha Franklin and Lisa Boyer had a pimp/hooker relationship. This theory was a way to explain how and why Boyer picked up Sam's clothes while fleeing the scene. It was a customary scam for a prostitute to get her unsuspecting john naked, then take off with his pants and shoes, or either ditch the clothes out of the motel window where someone in on the scam would grab them and run. In most cases the man would be too embarrassed to pursue the hooker. I actually wouldn't put it past Boyer and Franklin to have had a scam working in which Boyer rolled her johns, then broke off a piece of the action to Franklin. It's just that Sam considered staying in motels like the Hacienda well below his standards, and from all accounts he was much too street smart to fall for the old escape-with-the-pants-and-shoes routine.

Absolutely no one in my family believes Sam voluntarily checked into the Hacienda motel with Lisa Boyer, and his brothers and sisters will go to their graves saying that the idea of Sam raping one woman and attacking another in a cheap motel is preposterous. Maybe Sam was lured to the location, maybe he was taken there against his will, we can't say for certain. A motel like the Hacienda could've been a victim of extortion themselves, explaining why it ended up being the chosen location for such a crime.

What we do know is that Sam was made out to be a raving, out-of-control psychopath, hell-bent on kidnapping and raping one woman, and breaking down the door to attack another in a semi-naked rage. We know that some entity was angry enough at Sam to exploit every humiliating detail that would destroy his image, down to his last moment on earth fighting a middle-aged woman in a jacket and one shoe. Also, the family knows there is certain evidence that wasn't brought to light in any of the proceedings.

When my aunts and uncles first viewed Sam's body at the A.R. Leak Funeral Home in Chicago, they were horrified. Sam's face was badly bruised and there was a sizable lump on his forehead above his left eye:

Agnes: Both of his hands were broken. His ribs were broken. The skin was missing from his knuckles and his fingernails were raw and ragged.

David: Sam didn't take no shit, Sam was fighting. Sam was strong and boy, could he hit...

Agnes: …and would fight in a minute. I'm telling you, all the skin was off of all of his knuckles. The skin was *gone*.

David: Sam fought. That's why I know they had to kill him. He *fought*…

Whoever it was Sam encountered in his last hours, it wasn't the scar-free Bertha Franklin. Just as Sam Cooke had fought throughout his life, he fought to the death as well.

But what exactly happened?

Chapter Thirteen

The Mystery

"It's a shame. Sam Cooke died way too early."

"What do you mean?"

"I mean 33 was way too soon."

"Too soon?"

"Well…yes, he had so much more to give the world."

"Let's see, he was a singer, a songwriter, a producer and arranger. He owned his own record labels, his own music publishing company and his own management company. In addition to that, he was the first black artist to retain his own publishing rights with a major record label. Don't get me wrong, I agree his life was tragically cut short, but my point is he didn't need a whole lifetime to change music history. After all, Jesus changed history, and he died at 33 as well."

"Really?"

"Really."

–conversation between this author and a
Sam Cooke fan, November, 2002.

IF THIS EXCHANGE LEFT YOU feeling a little uneasy, relax. I'm not, in any shape, form, or fashion equating Sam Cooke to Jesus Christ. My point in this discussion was that even though Sam's life was relatively short, he was able to accomplish much more than most people accomplish in a full lifetime. I'd like to think that the physical being the world knew as Sam Cooke completed *God's* plan; it just so happens that the 33 year, 11 month project is well short of what's considered a normal lifespan in mortal comparison. It was obvious that even as a child singing to his popsicle-stick audience, Sam Cooke was destined for greatness, greatness he eventually went on to achieve. When Sam's mission was completed, God called His servant home.

I can't say for sure what really happened to Sam Cooke in the early-morning hours of December 11, 1964, nor can anyone in my family. What I can do, however, is share what I have pieced together from research, rumor, and talking to relatives about his character.

Because I'm a family member, you might expect me to make up excuses for the way Sam Cooke died instead of accepting the facts and testimonies as presented. You may feel it's only natural for me to find some other way to explain how Sam died, even if it meant subscribing to bizarre and outlandish theories, rather than face the truth that my uncle may have indeed died as reported. Yet as an author, my initial intent was to present the story from several points of view, state the pros and cons of all arguments, and let the reader decide from there.

However, during the course of my research, the scales of logic tipped heavily to one side. It became apparent that the explanations of how Sam died were so flawed, trying to justify the results of the *coroner's inquest* would be subscribing to the bizarre and outlandish. On the contrary, there were so many negative forces affecting Sam's life, negative forces that were prominent but not readily verifiable because of their ambiguity, that to not discuss their overwhelming influence would be the disservice. If someone wants to write a book supporting the findings of the LAPD and the Los Angeles County Coroner's Inquest, then God bless 'em. In the meantime, I'm going to stick by my theory that Sam Cooke did not die as reported and write about that.

I'm more inclined to believe Sam met with foul play either at PJ's or just after he left PJ's, and then somehow ended up at the Hacienda motel. Sam habitually lived his life with a high degree of style and class, and I ruled out the idea of him voluntarily checking into a sleazy motel. Taking it a step further, I ignored all testimonies from Lisa Boyer, Bertha Franklin, and Evelyn Card, and instead concentrated on events leading up to his arrival at the Hacienda.

Most explanations of Sam's death involve recreating the facts of the inquest instead of using scientific data to formulate a theory as to what may have happened. However, I did come across an article from a Forensic Pathologist who thought "outside the box" and made an attempt to dissect the coroner's autopsy report. The following excerpts are from an article called "Review of the Pathology Report" by Dr. Rodney Muhammad:

I believe that Sam was hit over the head at another location, transferred to the Hacienda, dragged from his car into Bertha's apartment (hence the ragged fingernails), dumped onto the floor and shot point blank by a professional who knew just where to place the pistol.

Normally a .22 does not have the power or the luck to do the kind of damage that this round did. However, if placed between the 3rd and 4th ribs at the mid-axillary line (under the armpit) at point-blank range, the small round avoided any collision with a rib bone or significant muscle tissue that would have kept it from penetrating both the lungs AND the heart. The shot also may have been timed to be fired on inhalation to further decrease the resistance.

The reason I feel he was struck on the head someplace else has to do with the amount of swelling that was noted at autopsy. If the blow was delivered as Bertha said, AFTER she shot him, the swelling would be insignificant because of two things: volume depletion of blood and fluid due to massive internal bleeding (not enough fluid left to make a head blow swell) and the heart had stopped pumping altogether which would result in an aborted inflammatory response…Also, no mention of how much rigor mortis had set in based on the police tapes and apparent time of death. This would have been useful in determining if a horrific struggle could have been between Sam and his real assassin as he struggled for his life.

Shortly after Sam's death, there was a buzz originating from restaurant patrons at Martoni's saying Sam received a "desperate" phone call from a male associate that night. Supposedly it was a matter of life and death for the person calling, and they begged Sam to meet them at PJ's. Since there have been endless rumors about what happened to Sam Cooke in his last hours, I took the story with a grain of salt. I never thought about the "phone call" theory again until I came across *L.A. Exposed*, written by Paul Young. In the book he briefly talks about Sam's murder, though the facts in his story are peppered with mistakes. What's interesting, however, is the footnote that accompanied the story:

When Fuller's uncle told the detectives that he thought the owners of PJ's had something to do with the murder, they told him, "Whoa, stop right there. You don't want to get involved with this, old man, it's bigger than you think."

The reference to PJ's made sense, but who was "Fuller?" I read and reread the article and it never mentioned "Fuller" or his uncle. Instead of shedding light on Sam's case, the footnote made me even more confused. It wasn't until I looked up "Fuller" in the book's index did I realize that Young intended the footnote to go to another story.

Bobby Fuller was the 23-year-old lead singer of a group called "The Bobby Fuller Four." He was best known for the hit song "I Fought the Law (and the Law Won)," and his band was regularly booked at PJ's. But on July 18, 1966 his body was found by his mother, dressed in pajamas and slumped over his car's front seat with the windows rolled up. When she opened the door, she was almost floored by heavy gasoline fumes. The interior of the car, as well as Bobby's clothes and hair, had been doused with gasoline. There was a book of matches and an open gas can on the front seat.

The L.A. County coroner's autopsy determined the cause of death as asphyxiation due to gasoline inhalation, and also concluded that gasoline had been poured on Fuller's clothes and down his throat *after* he had died. But despite the autopsy results, facial cuts, a broken finger, and massive bruises on his chest and shoulders as if he'd been beaten, the LAPD report ruled Bobby Fuller's death a suicide, citing "no evidence of foul play."

As if that weren't strange enough, Bobby's brother Randy Fuller said that Bobby received an urgent phone call in the early hours of the morning of the 18th, a call so disturbing he jetted out the door without even getting dressed. "Someone asked him to be somewhere," Randy said, "and he left right after that. No one knows where he went or why, but it was the last time he was seen alive." The mysterious caller was thought to be a waitress at PJ's named Melody who, despite turning tricks on the side, was the closest thing Bobby had to a girlfriend.

Fuller and his band were signed to Del-fi Records, and it was understood that the label's owner Bob Keane was aware of the impending break-up of the Bobby Fuller Four. The rumor was that Keane was indebted to mob-related investors who helped him start the label. It was thought that if these investors somehow found out that Keane had a $1 million life insurance policy on Bobby Fuller, they'd whack Fuller just to make sure Keane had the money to pay his debts.

So what does all of this have to do with Sam Cooke? Before Bob Keane owned Del-fi, he was the co-founder of Keen Records, the tiny label which made Sam Cooke an overnight success with its release of "You Send Me." Keen Records also released a second million-selling single, "Wonderful World," after Sam left the label and signed with RCA.

It has never been proven Bob Keane was instrumental in Bobby Fuller's death, and I have no evidence Keane ever took out a life insurance policy on Sam Cooke. But the stories about both singers receiving mysterious emergency phone calls, as well as both having links to Bob Keane and PJ's nightclub are eerily similar. The circumstances surrounding Bobby Fuller's death were on the same level of absurdity as those surrounding Sam Cooke's. In both cases, the police and coroner's reports differ greatly from one another and ignore key pieces of evidence. By the way, PJ's night-club was co-owned by the reputed East Coast mobster Dominic Lucci and the Lebanese-born L.A. kingpin Adel "Eddie Nash" Nasrallah.

Since Sam Cooke died just days before he planned to dissolve all ties with Allen Klein and J.W. Alexander, there have always been suspicions about their involvement as well. "Alexander was something!" Dot assessed. "I lost all respect for him. He was trying to get what he could for himself. He'd grin in your face and stab you in your back." As for Klein, it was always assumed he was in New York at the time of Sam's death, but his recollection of the facts during that critical time period invites more questions than it provides answers.

There are certain moments in one's life where time seems to stand still. For example, most Americans who are old enough to remember John F. Kennedy's assassination in November of 1963 could tell you exactly what they were doing when they received the news. Most of my generation can pinpoint their whereabouts when the World Trade Center collapsed in September of 2001. And to a person, my family members can recall exactly where they were and what they were doing when they first heard the news of Sam's death.

In Peter Guralnick's "Dream Boogie," Allen Klein says he first heard about Sam's death on the radio. "It was snowing hard in New York" was the reason Guralnick gave as to why Klein couldn't leave the city immediately. Whether the snow factor was Klein's recollection or Peter's assumption of why Klein couldn't leave the city is unclear. What is clear is that it had not snowed in New York City but that the city's outbound flights were crippled by a massive rain and fog system that extended all the way to the Midwest. The Coast Guard patrolling the area reported that the fog was so thick it caused a Dominican cargo ship to run aground off the Rockaway peninsula. Both Kennedy International Airport in New York and Newark Airport in New Jersey canceled flights due to heavy fog. The only problem with using the fog as an excuse, however, is that the delays and cancellations occurred Saturday, December 12th.

According to the U.S. Weather Bureau's forecast for December 11,

1964, New York City expected rain with milder temperatures, and the actual temperature did reach as high as 53F that day--hardly ideal conditions for a crippling snowstorm. Even going back to December 9th, the weather was described as "clear," and the December 10th forecast for New York City stated "precipitation probability near zero today," proving it never snowed during the period from December 9th through the 12th.

If Klein had indeed been a victim of the fog which impeded local airports on the 12th, then he wouldn't have been able to land in Los Angeles until Sunday, the 13th. But according to Guralnick, after learning of Sam's death on the radio, "(Klein) couldn't get a flight out until the next day"— the next day being Saturday the 12th. In Daniel Wolff's "You Send Me," he notes Allen Klein as being in town as guests gathered at the Cooke home on Saturday the 12th. Wolff's co-writer G. David Tenenbaum interviewed S.R. Crain about that Saturday gathering. Crain not only remembered Klein's appearance at the Cooke home, he also recalled how uneasy he felt about Klein taking Barbara into Sam's master bedroom and talking with her privately for over an hour.

Guralnick goes on to talk about how Barbara drove Sam's Rolls-Royce to the airport to pick Klein up, then offered to take him to lunch at Martoni's. However, a local newspaper reported that after collapsing upon the news of Sam's death, Barbara was kept under heavy sedation by her physician. In "You Send Me," Wolff confirms this by stating Barbara spent the days immediately following Sam's death so heavily sedated "she barely seemed to know where she was." Certainly she would not be fit to drive anywhere under those conditions, let alone dine afterward. Even if she could drive, she would've had to leave behind a house full of guests in order to pick up a man she barely knew, a man who could've easily taken a cab from LAX to the Cooke home. And why, of all places, would she suggest Martoni's to have lunch?

Perhaps the mistaken recollection of weather conditions and lunch dates means nothing. But what if Allen Klein had been in Los Angeles *before* Sam's death? Considering his business interest in Sam, why wasn't Klein's physical location on December 11th ever brought into question?

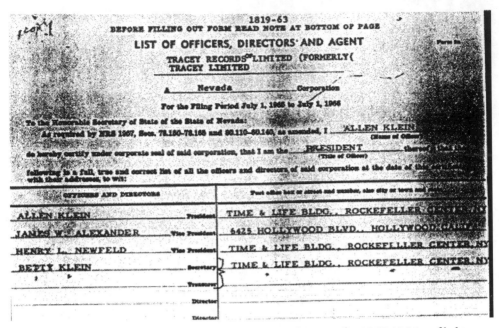

Tracey Limited's List of Officers, Directors, and Agent *for 1965-1966 as filed in Nevada in June of 1965 by Allen Klein.*

Regardless of his whereabouts, Klein saw an open door after Sam died and swiftly moved to take over his enterprises, renaming Tracey Limited to Tracey Records Limited less than a month after the funeral. The *List of Officers, Directors and Agent* for Tracey Records Limited for the filing period of July 1, 1965 to July 1, 1966, as filed by Allen Klein in June of 1965, listed himself as President, J.W. Alexander and business associate Henry Newfeld as Vice Presidents, and his wife, Betty Klein, as Secretary and Treasurer. The next year, J.W. Alexander was removed from office altogether, with Klein, Newfeld and wife Betty retaining their respective positions.

In March of 1970, Tracey Records Limited was one of several companies officially merged with ABKCO Industries Inc. to create the ABKCO-Klein Corporation. The merger included Cameo-Parkway Records (a Klein acquisition that sparked an SEC investigation), Sam's SAR Records and Malloy Music, and a few production companies associated with English bands but owned by ABKCO:

—Nanker Phlege Music, Ltd. (Rolling Stones)
—Eros International Corp. (The Dave Clark Five)
—Reverse Producers Corp. (Herman's Hermits)

Peter Noone of Herman's Hermits claims he wasn't worried about Klein's involvement with the band until the checks stopped coming. "1967 was the last statement we ever received," Noone said by e-mail. He remembers that Reverse Producers was designed to shelter the band from UK taxes, meaning the company was probably a carbon copy of Tracey Limited. The Dave Clark Five's Eros International was more than likely set up in the same manner.

"You know what? Some nights I get on that stage and I sweat. I look up and I've lost as much as 4 pounds during one performance. And I'll be damned if I let a white man get rich off of my sweat."

Sam wanted to ensure he didn't die like most black entertainers of his era, with his lifelong efforts lining the pockets of others. Yet in the end Sam's worst nightmare—what he had worked a lifetime to avoid and fought to the death to keep from coming true—had indeed become reality.

Sam had the presence of mind to set up a will, and made it a point to let Papa Cook know that his parents, brothers and sisters were all included. Roughly half of his estate was to go to Barbara and their children (supposedly there were provisions for his other children as well); the other half was to be split between his parents, siblings and a few close associates. Oddly enough, there's no record the will was ever registered officially, and Barbara claimed she never came across it. It would only make ethical sense, not common sense, for her to acknowledge an unregistered will since she would become administrator in its absence. There's strong evidence a will did exist from a January 1965 reference made in Jet magazine–"Sam Cooke's will is to be probated in Los Angeles County, Klein predicted"– and S. R. Crain was adamant for years at the fact Sam had a will. Not only had Crain seen it, he and Sam had discussed his inclusion. However, like so many other documents associated with Sam's business affairs, his will was never found and Barbara Cooke was in fact named administrator of Sam's estate.

Sam and Barbara in happier times, 1959.

(Photo courtesy of Toni Cook Howard)

Barbara was not above suspicion in Sam's death, and her peculiar actions only fueled notions of her involvement. Sam had been aware of her relationship with Bobby Womack, but the entrance they made at Sam's Los Angeles funeral caused a horrific gasp amongst the unsuspecting crowd. Arriving to the service in Sam's Rolls-Royce, Barbara and Bobby exited the car arm in arm—with Bobby dressed in the dead man's shirt, slacks and sport coat. Instead of being met with sympathy and condolences, the couple drew sneers, whispers of conspiracy, and looks of contempt and disgust.

Not humbled by the negative backlash from Sam's funeral, Barbara then asked Allen Klein to halt a private investigation into Sam's homicide, citing its results wouldn't bring her husband back anyway. Barbara's request immediately raised questions of a pre-meditated plot amongst an already doubtful public. If there had ever been a time to get to the bottom of exactly what happened, it was when the trail was hot and the story was at the height of public attention. But over the course of time the trail grew cold, interest waned, and Sam Cooke's legacy tarnished in absence of the truth.

If there were any doubts as to the nature of their relationship, Barbara agreed to marry Bobby Womack in February of 1965, despite being almost ten years his senior. Not only was their planned wedding date less than three months after Sam's death, the date was one day after Barbara was named administrator to Sam's estate. Since Bobby was only 20 years old, he needed the consent of his parents, who fortunately were not too blind to see how disgraceful the whole situation looked to the outside world. Denied the Womack's blessing, the couple had to wait until Bobby's 21st birthday in March and wed shortly thereafter. They had a son together and in disturbing fashion named him Vincent after Sam and Barbara's deceased son. Vincent Womack would eventually commit suicide as a young adult, citing a dysfunctional family unit as one of the factors in his decision. In 1985, Bobby would release one of his biggest R&B hits—a song called "I Wish He Didn't Trust Me So Much."

A lot of attention has focused on the events at the forefront (plans to leave Allen Klein, pending divorce from Barbara, etc.), but the background forces that had been turning up the heat on Sam over his last several months should not be overlooked. Had the "small dogs" broken their leash? The pressure Sam was under to comply with their extortion demands was not widely publicized, but was indeed very real. It was not out of the question these same forces were responsible for or worked in conjunction with whoever was behind Sam's death. It was also not out of the question they intended to exploit the gory details of his death as an example to those thinking of following Sam's footsteps.

Others such as Elvis Presley were resigned to the fact that it was Sam's open defiance and outspoken nature that helped seal his fate. For one thing, his close friendship with Muhammad Ali raised a lot of eyebrows. Sam always considered himself a Christian, but in private circles admitted he found some of the teachings of Islam interesting--most notably the importance of Black economic independence. In addition, Sam was constantly encouraging other artists to take charge of their own careers, repeatedly upsetting and embarrassing the powers that controlled the record industry both at the forefront and behind the scenes. Elvis Presley was quoted as asking "Why do you think Sam Cooke is dead?" to which his reply to his own question was "Everyone thinks he was murdered in a motel. Oh, he was murdered, all right. He was murdered because he got out of line. I got it from the horse's mouth. Cooke was told that he had a big mouth, to stay in line, and he didn't do it…You can only go so far."

I've come to accept the fact that to certain parties, Sam Cooke was worth more dead than alive. His strong cross-cultural appeal, immense popularity, and burgeoning power as a record executive attracted the attention (and envy) of those threatened by his potential, while at the same time his ever-present sense of independence and refusal to "stay in line" rubbed them the wrong way. Sam had invariably become a valuable pawn—a walking "rain check" if you will—to those who had a financial interest in him. This was important to note because there were some parties who were in a position to "cash in" on Sam Cooke in order to satisfy any debt, resentment, or personal greed.

Personally, I believe Sam was murdered at the Hacienda Motel, but not exactly as reported. From a valued source who will remain anonymous, I now have more faith in the following credible (though unproven) re-creation of events than I do the version that was officially reported:

It is my understanding that Sam Cooke was intentionally drugged while dining earlier in the evening. It is also my understanding that he did not drive his Ferrari to the Hacienda Motel under his own accord, but was instead driven there by someone else for an arranged "meeting." The agenda that night was to convince Sam—if not verbally, then physically—to take his career in a different direction. If he refused to comply, he was to be murdered in the motel room where his body would be discovered the next morning. The story in the newspapers would read that while spending time with a prostitute, Soul singer Sam Cooke had been robbed and killed. The horrific details of Sam's death would serve to "take him down a peg" through embarrassment and humility, while at the same time allow the vengeful parties to take advantage of any monetary rewards his absence might generate. But because of Sam's spirited nature, things that night didn't go as smoothly as planned.

While in the Hacienda motel room, an impaired Sam Cooke not only refused to comply with his captors, he became combative to the point he had to be beaten and eventually subdued with a blunt object to the head. During this altercation, it is possible Sam's hands were severely broken from fighting back, or from trying to protect his head from the blow(s). Semi-conscious and bewildered, most of his clothes were removed to create the scenario of a sleazy "sex-capade." He was then shot inside the motel room and left for dead.

It wasn't planned for Sam Cooke to ever leave the motel room that night, and certainly it wasn't planned for him to leave alive. But he stumbled out of the room in a daze, semi-clothed and looking for help, wounded but not necessarily bleeding; the small caliber bullet was meant to do more internal than external damage. While trying to make his way to the manager's office, he was spotted by several patrons of the motel. Sam asks the onlookers for help but receives none, for it was already understood by them that they were not to interfere. According to my source, all witnesses that night had been paid off, including Bertha Franklin who eventually died in Los Angeles in 1989. Perhaps this revelation explains the lack of credible eyewitnesses in this case.

Continuing to Franklin's office, Sam knocks loudly and repeatedly at her door, but to his despair there is no answer. His original killer, now aware his work had not been completed, is forced to drag Sam inside the manager's apartment and finish the job there. One gunshot bounces wildly off the ceiling and may have been intended to show evidence of a struggle. The other shot, more than likely the one Dr. Muhammad describes in his review of the autopsy report, proves to be fatal for Sam Cooke.

Since the murder scene is now the motel manager's office and not the motel room itself, the broken down door, blood stained dress, and disheveled room were all fabricated in order to create a self-defense alibi for Franklin. "The whole thing was like a movie," is how my source describes the staged cover-up. The flimsy stick seems to have been the best prop available to explain the large, swollen lump on the back of Sam's head, the lump that was allegedly inflicted in the earlier scuffle in the motel room.

Unfortunately I don't have much physical evidence to support my source's testimony, but because of this account, the answers given in the coroner's inquest seem to take on a different light. When one explores the possibility that Sam had something slipped into his food, for example, it's interesting to note how the inquest investigation avoids addressing the matter directly.

Autopsy Physician Dr. Harold Kade testified that Sam's blood "was submitted for chemical analysis for the presence of alcohol," and that his blood alcohol level was 0.14%—almost twice the 0.08% level at which a person could be considered legally drunk. Dr. Kade was then asked by the coroner "was there ever any evidence of narcotics?" (a vague question in itself), to which Kade's eloquent response was "There was no indication of recent needle puncture marks, and the findings were not suggestive of a narcotic overdose or narcotics in significant quantity at the time of death." In other words, there weren't enough drugs in Sam's system to say he died from a drug overdose.

But what *was* in Sam's system? We knew Sam's blood alcohol content. If his blood had been tested for narcotic substances, why weren't the contents of Sam's bloodstream either requested by the coroner during questioning or voluntarily disclosed by the autopsy physician? Did the coroner feel this information would add speculation to what he already saw as an "open and shut" case? After all, revealing the results of a quantitative narcotics test would have established if Sam had been drugged. If he had indeed been drugged, then the case may have gone to trial as a premeditated murder rather than ruled closed as a justifiable homicide. By the same token, could there have been a concerted effort not to make the contents of Sam Cooke's bloodstream public information? If my source's information is accurate, then that would certainly be a possibility.

Despite the results of Dr. Kade's blood alcohol report, Lisa Boyer testified "I don't believe he was drunk...I am sure he had one or two, but I am sure that he wasn't drunk," when asked if she thought Sam was under the influence of alcohol. Whether Dr. Kade's test results were over-exaggerated or Lisa Boyer was asked a question she couldn't truthfully answer, the number of conflicting testimonies left unchallenged in this inquest is mind-boggling.

The inquest also left me perplexed as to how the murderer's gun was fired three times yet only two bullets were found on the murder scene—the ricochet off the ceiling that ended up on the couch and the bullet that ended up in Sam Cooke. If my source is correct, then the missing bullet—the *first* bullet—was not fired in Franklin's apartment at all, but in the motel room. My initial thought was that this would contradict the autopsy report of finding only one bullet wound in Sam, and that the idea of the report overlooking a detail this fundamental would be absurd. However, taking into account that the autopsy physician may have concentrated solely on the noticeable wound (in itself only a 1/8" x 3/16" opening), and taking into account this was the same coroner's office that left so many obvious questions unanswered, the department's omission of another crucial fact in this inquest doesn't seem so out of the ordinary.

Also, the sequence of events inside the motel room is consistent with Dr. Muhammad's theory that Sam was hit over the head before he was shot. The sizable head knot noted in the autopsy report was clear evidence that internal bleeding had not yet occurred, and if an oversight to this magnitude is possible, then it may indeed be possible that a second bullet and/or bullet wound was overlooked as well. Only a re-opening of Sam's case and a subsequent exhumation of the body would answer that question completely.

Again, I cannot substantiate my source's Hacienda account personally, and as a result I am not inclined to say who was in the motel room with Sam. However, I do believe that the chilling details of this testimony are a more accurate portrayal of events than the "official" explanation contained in the coroner's report.

After the coroner's inquest, Barbara and the Cook family came to the agreement that there was a need for two funerals, one in Chicago and one in Sam's final resting place, Los Angeles. The Chicago visitation was held at the A.R. Leak Funeral Home on one of the coldest days of the year. The December wind-chill factor took the temperature to -20 F, yet the weather didn't seem to deter a turnout estimated in the tens of thousands. Mournful fans stood crying in the cold for hours, lined along Cottage Grove Avenue as far as the eye could see, in order to view the body. Those lucky enough to make their way inside the funeral home were bunched so tightly, the lobby's front window pane shattered from the pressure, sending shards of glass everywhere. The funeral was held at Tabernacle Missionary Baptist Church and the crowd there was just as dense. Agnes remembers the Chicago funeral this way:

"It was a madhouse! There were five funeral cars that held the family members and the children. My mother and dad were in the first car, and they let the first car unload. But when the second car tried to unload, people broke the line and rushed the car. The police couldn't hold them back because it was so many people. It was wall-to-wall people and so cold. They even broke the doors of the church pushing their way through."

"Jerry (childhood friend and policeman, Jerry Blades) just started swinging his nightstick, that's how we got through. If it weren't for Jerry, I don't think we would've even been able to get in the church. It was just a sea of people. They had to lift the children above the crowd and pass them along like sacks of potatoes. It was really something."

"The crowd picked one lady up and walked her out of her shoes! A brand new pair of shoes, she never found them, (they were) just left there where she stood... People were crying everywhere because Sam was one of them, born and raised in the neighborhood. It was so cold, you wouldn't think there would be that many people out there, but the crowd was blocks-long. Muhammad Ali was there, but I was in a fog (pausing for several seconds)…I really couldn't tell you who else was there. We had just seen the body for the first time, with his hands broken and all. It was just so emotional."

In a separate interview, my mom said this:

"What I remember is the people converging on us as we got out of the limousine. My feet never touched the ground from the car to the inside of the church. The crowd was packed so tightly, they lifted my body up off the ground and I was carried with the crowd as they moved toward the church. We eventually made it into the door, I don't know how...the crowd was so thick, it was totally unbelievable."

"I really don't remember anything about the service itself, because I was in a state of disbelief Sam was gone. I do remember passing his casket and seeing his hands. They had his hands folded across his body. I just started crying because it was so apparent that he fought so hard, the skin was off his hands. His knuckles were all torn up. All I could think about was how much he must have fought, and I just cried. It was so devastating because I couldn't believe he was gone. I really couldn't believe Sam was gone."

In addition to the grief my family endured, they also had to contend with the various rumors, innuendos, and accusations buzzing around the South Side of Chicago. Attempts to defend Sam's honor were futile due to the gruesome details of the case and lack of evidence to the contrary. The older Cooks found themselves defending Sam in social circles, and the children were narrowly avoiding fist fights at school. Once again, Papa Cook stepped forward and became the guiding influence for the family:

Renee: In honor of my grandfather a lot of (talk about Sam's death) was dropped. My grandfather sat me down and said "You have to understand you can never change what people think, no matter what you say, no matter what you do. You can voice your opinion, but you also have the choice of walking away." And I had to learn from that. Yes, a lot of things bothered me, but I had to learn to walk away.

Doncella: Sam's death was very traumatic for the family. Trying to convince everyone else about how he lived, how he died...I think about all the different arguments and confrontations family members got into following Sam's death. I remember Toni's mother (L.C.'s late wife, Barbara) standing in line at the grocery store. People were talking and she knew they didn't know what they were talking about. It takes everything within you to be quiet. But Papa had said "leave it alone," and we had no choice but to leave it alone.

Gene: As young men in the family, our uncles had a great influence on us. Not one of my uncles ever mistreated a woman in front of me. They've always taught us to treat a woman with respect and dignity. So I know for a fact that there's nothing in the world, nothing (Lisa Boyer) could have that would make my uncle behave that way.

Gwen: We knew, because we lived with Sam and we saw all the women, and men, really, that would flock to him. So for him to have gone after someone of the caliber of this person, we knew better, but we could not convince the world. We discussed it in a family forum, and when my grandfather said "you cannot change the minds of people, they're going to believe what they want to believe," it was hard, but we had to accept the fact that Papa said "just leave it alone." It was the hardest thing in the world not to defend my beloved uncle, but my grandfather said "leave it alone" and we did.

Doncella: People who knew Sam knew without a doubt that it wasn't like it was reported. And *they* defended him! When your family jumps to your defense, people say "that's just his family." But when others do, people tend to listen more. There are people all over who took our cross and joined our crusade…

After the Chicago funeral, Sam's body was flown back to Los Angeles where his final services were held at Mount Sinai Baptist Church. Traffic was backed up for several blocks as the crowd of over 5,000 mourners, more than triple the church's designated capacity, methodically made the trek to Mount Sinai. Along the way, Sam's music could be heard blaring from windows throughout the neighborhood as local radio stations paid homage to the slain singer. As if scripted for the occasion, ominous clouds and a slight drizzle enveloped what would normally be a sunny Southern California sky.

The line-up slated to perform on the program read like a who's who among gospel, blues and popular music entertainers. Sam's enormous popularity pushed the 1500-seat church past its limits and speakers had to be set up outside for the many people who couldn't make their way in. Despite the talents of Billy Preston on organ and electrifying performances by Lou Rawls and Bobby Blue Bland, what should've been an uplifting homecoming was anything but. The unexpected death of such a young, vibrant pioneer, especially taking into account the circumstances, created a dismal atmosphere of shock and disbelief.

Hysterical actions seemed to be the norm more than the exception for the day. Besides Barbara and Bobby's jaw-dropping entrance, a distraught Zelda Sands got into a car accident en route. Arriving late as a result, she was almost denied entrance into the services, and ended up punching and kicking her way past the church ushers to get inside. "I was so beside myself," she recalls, "that even *after* the funeral, I got lost."

An obviously-intoxicated Johnnie Morisette, who arrived at the funeral in the Cadillac Eldorado Sam bought him as a birthday present, interrupted the program by wailing over the casket "Sam, I'm sorry! I'm so sorry, Sam, please forgive me!" in a manner that curiously seemed more guilt-ridden than grief-stricken.

After stirring eulogies from newspaper columnist Gertrude Gibson and Mount Sinai's Pastor, gospel singer Bessie Griffin was supposed to close out the program but was too anguished to perform. As the restless crowd stirred with anticipation, someone yelled out "Brother Ray is in the house!", "Brother Ray is in the house!" in reference to the legendary Ray Charles' attendance as a regular mourner. Unprepared and unrehearsed, the blind singer was led to the piano where he sat down and whispered into the microphone in a voice that cracked with emotion, *"Sam, baby, this one's for you,"* and proceeded to belt out the traditional spiritual "Angels Watching Over Me." The performance sent chills through every soul in the church and silenced the streets outside. Needless to say, there wasn't a dry face in the house, including that of Brother Ray. On a rainy Saturday afternoon filled with sadness, sorrow, and uncertainty, Ray Charles managed to send Sam off in grand fashion after all.

Sam was laid to rest at Forest Lawn Memorial Park in Glendale, California. His plot is located in the privately-accessible *Garden of Honors* (son Vincent rests in *Lullabyland*), and on his gravesite is a simple bronze marker that depicts a couple staring at the sun rising over a distant mountain:

Sam Cooke
I Love You
1930-1964
Until the Day Break,
And the Shadows Flee Away

In what can only be described as bitter irony, the serenity of the message is eclipsed by the incorrect year of his birth. The irony is that "Sam Cooke" should be a household name, yet his musical legacy seems to have been eclipsed by the incorrect details of his death. Sam Cooke did not die in shame, but died a hero fighting for justice. One of the greatest entertainers, humanitarians, record industry pioneers and effervescent personalities who ever lived should be familiar to anyone who has been a fan of pop music over the last forty years, yet many Americans can't identify him unless you give them a song title or hum a few bars of one of his classics.

I sincerely believe that Sam Cooke was put on this earth for a reason. The fact that he continues to touch the lives of people around the globe more than forty years after his death is a testament to how special an individual he truly was. To listen to Charles describe how Sam was so talented in so many fields gave me a sense of the tremendous amount of respect and admiration he had for his younger brother. The fact that my mother can still sing the "Indian Song" Sam taught her is proof that his impact on her as a young girl has lasted well into her adult life. Joe Cook still basks in the warmth exuded from "the only man I called Dad." More than fifty years later Dot's voice still resonates with romance as she recalls times spent with Sam. For her to unconsciously say "we've never, ever stopped being together," as if his physical being were still with us here on Earth, is overwhelming evidence that Sam's spirit lives on and remains strong despite his absence. After a person is gone you might not always remember everything that person did, and you might not always remember everything that person said, but you will always remember the way that person made you feel—Sam Cooke always made those closest to him feel special, important, and loved.

Too much attention has been placed on how Sam died and not enough on the incredible life he lived. It has taken more than forty years for the ugly tarnish of his death to wear off so that the wondrous beauty of his legacy could shine through. Now that it has, we should embrace it and realize that we may never see anything like it again in our lifetime. Let us not dwell on the way we lost Sam or how short his time on Earth was, but instead be grateful for the almost thirty-four years he did give us. I was never fortunate enough to have spent time with my uncle, but I know that one day I'll meet him at the Crossroads. Until that time comes, I dedicate this book in honor of his loving memory.

Sam, baby, this one's for you.

Chapter Fourteen

The Aftermath

AFTER SAM'S CHICAGO FUNERAL, HIS family met at his parent's South Side home on 83rd and Maryland. As with any family get-together, Mama Cook provided a glorious array of food which was spread from one end of the dining room table to the other, though the occasion this day was anything but festive. Congregating for a meal is the standard procedure anytime there's a loss in the Cook family. It has always symbolized our family's unity; though we may choose to grieve privately and individually, it is a reminder that there are always other shoulders to cry upon in our darkest hour. After my great-grandmother's passing in 1967, her daughters carried on the tradition and took turns as the family hostess. Holiday dinners and post-funeral repasts are now held at Agnes', the youngest and last remaining Cook daughter.

Barbara Cooke attended the Chicago funeral. As Sam's wife she was welcomed into the Cook home, and while her demeanor reflected understandable stress, her behavior was still strange to say the least. My Aunt Phyllis remembers things this way:

"When Barbara came over to Mama Cook's house, she was a nervous wreck. She handed Charles a list of things she wanted him to bring back; the car, some clothes he had, things of that nature. She also told him 'of course you know Sam paid your mother's life insurance, and you're going to need to take care of that, because I'll no longer be paying it.' She was just cold and insensitive. Why bring something like that up now? Then she started talking crazily. She asked 'Did anyone say that they saw my car at the motel?' Everyone's response was 'What are you talking about?' Our minds were not on anything other than the grief we were going through. Between the anger and the frustration, it was very easy to miss something that was being said, but I do remember her asking the question 'Did anyone say that they saw my car at the motel?'"

My mother, David, and Charles were not within earshot, but my Aunt Agnes confirmed Barbara's question and seemed amazed she had forgotten about it:

"Oh, yes she did say that! After she said it, the only way we could make sense of why Sam would've gone to that motel was that maybe he was driving by and saw Barbara's car in the parking lot. Or maybe it was her twin sister, Beverly, because she used to drive Barbara's car. Barbara used to hang out in the lounge across the street. Maybe Sam drove by there and saw the car and stopped. But that's just speculation; we were just throwing ideas around as far as how he could've ended up at that motel."

Personally, I still believe foul play occurred between PJ's and the Hacienda motel, and that Sam's scraped-up knuckles, broken hands, and swollen forehead were the results of a terrific struggle on his part. The ragged fingernails may have indeed come from Sam being forcefully dragged (possibly into Bertha's apartment) as Dr. Muhammad suggested, and I support his conclusion that the amount of swelling at the back of the head indicated the blow occurred before he was shot. A battle of this intensity clearly didn't occur with Bertha Franklin, but with a more formidable opponent or opponents. However, I still find it very interesting Barbara would be concerned about her car being seen at (not around, according to how she phrased the question) the Hacienda motel. Had she been at the scene of the crime? Could this explain why she asked Allen Klein to halt an investigation into Sam's murder?

It was during this same visit Barbara asked a special request of the Cook family:

"The day after Sam's funeral, Barbara wanted Mama, Papa and all the sisters and brothers to sign a power of attorney of Sam's estate over to her," David recalls. "She said 'I can't do anything without all of your signatures.'"

"We wouldn't sign it because she wouldn't give us a copy to give to our attorney first," Agnes adds. "She went back to California and we haven't been asked anything about it since then. She kept saying she couldn't do nothing without all of our signatures."

"That's what she said," David agrees. "If you could've seen the look on her face…When she left out of here, there was a look on her face—scared."

"She was desperate," Agnes states. "She was pleading and begging with us to sign it. I said 'We can't sign this, Barbara. We don't even know what we're signing.' She wouldn't even let us see what the papers said! She just wanted to show us where to sign."

"If there wasn't a will, there was something Sam had incorporated," Agnes continued. "Otherwise, Barbara wouldn't have been saying she couldn't do nothing without the Cook family. I think Sam had all of us—his parents, brothers and sisters—listed in some capacity in his companies, and she was trying to get us to relinquish all of our rights, but we wouldn't do it. That was the end of that incident. We never heard anything more from her about it. Not only would she not give us the papers, she wouldn't even let us *see* them! We never signed anything, but somehow she came away with power of attorney over Sam's estate anyway."

Needless to say, Barbara's December 1964 visit left a bad taste in the mouths of the Cook family. They had always respected her as Sam's wife, but in their hearts hoped Sam would marry Dot Holloway. Dot was extremely close to Sam's parents, brothers and sisters—especially my grandmother. Before Sam's death however, my mother had requested the presence of Sam's daughters for her June 1965 Chicago wedding to my father: Tracey as a flower girl and Linda as a hostess. Barbara and husband Bobby Womack drove from California to Chicago six months after Sam's funeral, and the family was suspicious because they hadn't heard from Barbara after she said she desperately needed their signatures to free up frozen assets. Also, the fact that Bobby Womack showed up to Sam's Los Angeles funeral in Sam's car and clothes never set well with the Cook brothers either. The following excerpts are from a conversation about that awkward, tension-filled visit:

David: (Talking to me) You weren't around when me and Charles kicked Bobby's ass.

Agnes: You weren't even born yet. It was Gwen's wedding. They brought Tracey in to be in the wedding.

Gwen: What was that, like six months later? Yeah, it was six months later, because Sam got killed in December, and my wedding was in June.

Agnes: See, Gwen had already asked them could Tracey be a flower girl, so I've got to give her credit; she had a lot of heart, because she drove all the way here from California.

David: Me and Charles were riding around. Charles said "man, you know what? He's got a lot of nerve coming here. We should go there and kick his ass." I said 'yeah, you're right, Charles.'

Agnes: They were staying at the Roberts Motel… how did y'all find out what room they were in, though?

David: We went to the desk. They knew us and they told us which room they were in. Hell, they even knew why we were there. Charles knocked on the door. Bobby said "who is it?", and Charles said "Charlie Cook." Bobby said "wait a minute," because they had a gun. Charles came in and started whooping Bobby, and Barbara went for the gun. I grabbed Barbara and she bit the shit out of my finger. That's when I said "Charlie, she's got a gun!", so I twisted her around away from him so she couldn't fire. Charlie looked at her and said "Are you crazy?" He took the gun and whipped *both* their butts with it. He made them both sit on the bed, side by side, and whipped the shit out of them!

Agnes: The police came and got them and brought Barbara to the police station and told her she had to go in there and identify them. She said "I ain't going in there with them crazy Cooks, they'll kill me!" She refused to identify them so they had to let them go.

Gwen: David was in my wedding, and this was the night before. My mama said "girl, get some sleep!" I said "Mama, I can't sleep, I *can't* sleep!"

David: Boy, we really kicked their butts, no, no; *Charles* really kicked their butts!…

Tracey and Linda had spent the night over my grandmother's house and participated in the wedding as planned. Bobby and Barbara did not attend. Sam had planned to send my mother and father on a week-long trip to Jamaica for their honeymoon, but never got a chance to make the reservations.

Barbara Cooke spent the next year and a half unsuccessfully attempting to take control of Sam's business entities by wielding her newly-found power over his estate. She wrestled back and forth with J.W. Alexander over day-to day operation issues, and at one point threatened to dissolve both record labels and publishing companies entirely. She repeatedly turned down Alexander's attempts to buy her out (the status of Crain's shares was unknown at this point). Instead, in April of 1966 she sold her share of the publishing rights to Sam's old producers at RCA, Hugo Peretti and Luigi Creatore, for a mere $103,000. Within a year Hugo & Luigi had sold the rights to Allen Klein for an undisclosed amount. J. W. Alexander, in a financial bind of his own, realized the walls were closing in and eventually sold his share of the publishing rights to Klein as well.

The sale of Alexander's rights symbolized the fall of the last pillar of financial and artistic control the three gospel veterans established but failed to maintain. Allen Klein was now the sole owner all of Sam's enterprises, much to the dismay of the Cook family:

"What makes me mad is that Barbara *knew* the last thing Sam wanted to do was give up control of his music and have a white man take over," Agnes laments. "That's what hurts. I feel worse about that than anything concerning his death. What she did destroyed everything he worked so hard to build. Everybody close to Sam knew he never wanted that."

In a separate interview, David shared the same sentiments:

"What irks me is that Sam strove so hard to be an independent black businessman, then to let a white man take over, that really hurts. Sam was such an astute businessman. I can't believe Barbara came along and signed the whole thing away for $100,000."

In a one-on-one interview with Charles, I asked him if he resented how things turned out:

"Hell yeah, I resent it! I don't like that shit! But you've got to give it to (Klein); he was smart enough to buy it. I blame Barbara. Barbara was the cause of the whole thing, giving it away for $100,000."

"Something paltry," I added.

"Hell, yeah!" His voice reflected disgust at just the thought of the whole matter. "Shit!"

I was curious how Hugo & Luigi ever got involved in the negotiations in the first place. According to Wolff, Hugo & Luigi made it seem as if they were working on the West Coast, just happened to give Barbara a call, and ended up buying Sam's publishing rights from her. After a year, they sold their share to Allen Klein because of "legal complications with Alexander's ownership." To me, it all seemed a little too convenient.

As I suspected, Allen Klein's association with Hugo & Luigi went back several years. Two of Klein's early associates were guitarist Buddy Knox and bassist Jimmy Bowen of the Texas group *Rhythm Orchids*. Knox and Bowen were signed to Roulette Records, owned by the infamous Morris Levy. Levy, who had reputed ties to the Genovese crime family, was one of the biggest swindlers of artist royalties in music history. He owned a huge music publishing catalog and among other travesties, had been accused of attaching his name as songwriter to hits like Frankie Lymon's "Why Do Fools Fall in Love." Hugo & Luigi became co-owners of Roulette after purchasing the shares of co-founder George Goldner, and they undoubtedly met Klein through Knox and Bowen if not earlier. If there was one thing the duo could've learned from Levy, it was that a publishing catalog like Sam Cooke's had significant value. It's possible their visit with Barbara and their sale of Sam's publishing rights to Allen Klein may have been more calculated than coincidental.

Whatever the case, one flattering aspect following Sam's death was the tremendous amount of recognition his music legacy garnered. After closing out 1964 with a record three #1 singles from the same album, The Supremes released their rendition of eleven Cooke-written hits on "We Remember Sam Cooke" in April of 1965. Otis Redding, Smokey Robinson, Marvin Gaye, Keith Richards, Rod Stewart, Roberta Flack and Solomon Burke were all influenced by Sam throughout the mid '60's and into the '70's. Al Green even admitted he tried to sound like Sam Cooke on some of his earlier albums.

Sam's music languished in the '70's as hostile contractual disputes between Allen Klein and RCA left the listening public with only mediocre compilations, the best being RCA's "This is Sam Cooke" in 1970. Klein owned the rights to the songs Sam recorded in the last year of his life, most notably the classic "A Change is Gonna Come." Klein denied its inclusion in any project that didn't meet his approval and as a result the song never made an album appearance throughout the entire decade. The disagreement ran so deeply and the quality of available material was so poor, RCA only put out three Cooke compilations between 1977 and 1984—and one of those was the 1978 re-release of "Sam Cooke at the Copa." This multi-year power struggle over Sam's catalog was reminiscent of the Specialty/Keen feud and probably had Sam turning over in his grave. In 1985 RCA finally released "Live at the Harlem Square Club, 1963," and the following year the two sides reached common ground on "The Man and His Music," blessing the listening public with the most complete Cooke anthology to that point.

The Cook family wouldn't have much association with Barbara in the 20 years after she sold her publishing rights. Within that period her marriage to Bobby Womack fizzled, and she married several more times, including a brief union with ex-Highway QC Lee Richard. My parents and I did spend a couple of hours at her house on a California road trip in 1972, but other than that there wasn't much interaction with the Cook family. Surprisingly, the family's next encounter with the West Coast Cookes would not be with Barbara, but with her oldest daughter, Linda.

Visit to Barbara's California home, August, 1972. (a) Gwen and Linda.

(b) clockwise: Tracey, Barbara, Gwen and Linda.

The Cook children, 1974: Top row, Hattie, Agnes, Mary, L.C. Charles and David. Papa Cook is seated in the dark shirt, flanked by his cousin and brother.

(Photos courtesy of Gwendolyn Greene)

In the winter of 1982, Linda Cooke began a nationwide crusade to meet all of Sam's out-of-wedlock children. Initially they were flattered because there had never been any interaction between themselves and the children Sam had with Barbara. Unfortunately, it turned out Linda's intent was anything but sentimental. Sam's daughter, Sharon Cooke, remembers things this way:

"(Linda) called me and said she was staying at a hotel in Oakland and she wanted to meet me. I had always wanted to meet her as well, and she suggested we spend the weekend together. The next day she called me and asked was I alone and could she come to my apartment. She said she wanted me to join the Sam Cooke Publishing Company. I thought I was going to be a part of a family thing put together on behalf of my father and all his kids. That's what I thought I was signing. Little did I know she had me sign over my power of attorney to her for the sale of my father's (publishing) catalog. I didn't really read it because it was in legal jargon, but I believed what she told me. She gave me $500 and after I signed the papers, all of a sudden she had to go. No weekend, no spending time together, all the plans she had told me about went out the window."

"Personally, I'm tired of the whole situation. I've had attorneys that tried to find her but every time I try to go after what she took from me, they get started on the case then mysteriously quit. It always came to a dead end. But I've given it to God and I'm through. She told me I was going to get royalties from the company and everything, but when I met her, it wasn't about any money; I just wanted my sister in my life. Then after finding out how she was, I haven't talked to her since, nor do I want to."

Sam's daughters Paula Jackson and Sharon Cooke. (Photo courtesy of Richard Nichols)

Daughter Paula Jackson tells a similar story:

"Linda called me and I was excited to hear from her; I mean, this was my sister and we had never met each other. I agreed to meet her in a hotel near downtown (Chicago). She was there with L.C. and her husband Cecil. She told me they wanted to get a publishing company together with all the kids, and that she wanted me and the rest of Sam's kids to sign this paper to join this company from our father. There was no lawyer there; the only one I really knew in the room was L.C. I looked to him for some sort of direction, but he just sat in the corner not saying anything. After I signed the papers, I left but was kind of disappointed because I thought we were gonna spend more time together."

"It just so happened I had planned to visit my girlfriend in California a couple of months after that and told her I wanted to drop by the (publishing company's) office. Her husband was in show business and she kept telling me she had a bad feeling about the whole thing and that I shouldn't visit the office. All I kept saying was 'this is my family, she's my sister.' When I got there I went to the front desk and said 'Hi. I'm Paula Jackson!' I was supposed to own a piece of the company, so I figured they'd recognize the name, but they looked at me like I was crazy. I asked was Linda in and they said 'no' like she didn't come in on a regular basis and then they asked me again who I was. That's when I realized my girlfriend was right, I shouldn't have come. I got so embarrassed, I just left."

Fortunately, Paula was able to obtain a copy of the document she signed. The fact that Sam Cooke Publishing's address and suite number is exactly the same as the law firm who prepared the documents instantly throws up a red flag upon close inspection, but like her sister, Paula signed the form out of the excitement of being included in a Cooke family project. Having never grown up with their father, both Paula and Sharon cherished what they felt was the next best recognition–Linda's acknowledgment as family.

Neither sister realized that in 1985 the original copyrights of Sam's music catalog were set to expire, and that the Sam Cooke Publishing Company was set up take control of the copyrights once they did. By signing the Agreement, Paula granted the Sam Cooke Publishing Company power of attorney to represent her interest in the catalog's ownership. Less than three years later, a letter dated September 25, 1985 was supposedly mailed to her saying that the sale of the Sam Cooke Publishing Company had begun and that by signing the enclosed release, she would receive a check for $7,000 after applicable fees. The buyer of the Sam Cooke Publishing Company was none other than ABKCO Industries.

Paula claims she never received nor signed the release to agree to the sale of Sam Cooke Publishing to ABKCO, nor did she ever receive the $7,000 check. Like Sharon, her legal attempts to resolve the issue had been unsuccessful:

"The only time I signed anything was to agree to be in the Sam Cooke Publishing Company. They have my signature on the release form, as well as my endorsement on the check. I signed one piece of paper one time, but they have my signature on three pieces of paper. The only money I received was $500 when I met Linda at the hotel."

"What hurts most is that my father set something aside for all of us (tears starting to form). Linda got a chance to spend time with him, she got a chance to live in the nice house with all the nice things, we never got none of that. And then for her to take away the little he did leave for us really hurts. All of us (the out-of-wedlock children) have had to struggle all our lives, and I know that's not what my father intended."

An angry Paula Jackson confronted Allen Klein at a June 2003 Chicago release party for Sam's new line of Super Audio CD's. She told him how she had only received $500 from her father's estate in all of 39 years. She explained she was in a financial bind and that there had to be something more her father had left. In August of 2003, ABKCO faxed Paula copies of the Sam Cooke Publishing Company Trust Agreement she signed, as well as the signed waiver release for the company's sale to ABKCO and the endorsed $7,000 cancelled check dated October 15, 1986, as if to say ABKCO had no further obligation to her financial situation. Paula responded by saying this was the first time she had seen the release or the check, and that neither signature was hers. Without admitting error on their part, ABKCO Music, Inc. quietly sent Paula a check for $7,000 dated September 5, 2003.

Sam's daughter Denise Somerville is deceased, and his son, Keith Bolling, could not be reached for comment

In late 1985, Papa Cook received a letter from the newly-formed Rock and Roll Hall of Fame stating that Sam Cooke was one of its initial inductees. The January 1986 induction ceremony was held in New York City and all of the Cooke siblings attended, as did Sam's widow, Barbara Cooke. Barbara had been in and out of Chicago several times in the 20-plus years since Sam's funeral, but their meeting in New York City marked the first time the family had any prolonged interaction with her, and unfortunately it wasn't a joyous reunion.

After the induction ceremony, as the Cook family was leaving the Awards dinner, Barbara approached Agnes and asked what the family's plans were for the rest of the evening. Agnes said they didn't have anything planned, but that Charles, David, Mary and Hattie were going to meet in the suite her and my grandmother shared. Barbara asked could she tag along and Agnes said she didn't mind. Dot didn't attend the Awards dinner, but was waiting in the suite when the family returned.

"Barbara came in the room with Charles," she recalls. "When she came into the room, she looked at me and said 'who are *you*?', but before I could answer, she joined the conversation talking about Sam. Barbara broke in with 'his mother didn't take care of him anyway,' which we knew was a lie because Mother Cook was a wonderful mother."

Barbara then proceeded to bring up Sam and the Hacienda motel. Agnes told her she never believed Sam voluntarily checked into the Hacienda, to which Barbara disagreed, then added "He wasn't no good no way," much to the surprise of the whole Cook clan. Hattie responded by saying "What do you mean he wasn't no good? He took care of your lazy ass!" As if she hadn't gone far enough, Barbara then answered with a reference to Hattie's status as a mother of seven children. Agnes paused, waiting for the response that never came from her older sister. "I wanted Hattie to hit her. Heck, *I* wanted to hit her!"

"Barbara was yelling 'just go on and kill me, just go on and kill me!'" David recalls. "She *wanted* her ass kicked!"

"I was mad at Hattie because she didn't hit her," Agnes states, her anger rekindling. "How is it you've got two brothers and two sisters in a room…"

"It was three sisters." David corrects.

"Yeah, three sisters. *And* Dot! And you're going to tell them their deceased brother was no damn good? I don't know why she even wanted to come back to the room if she wasn't going to do nothing but talk about Sam."

"Sometimes people want to be punished," Gwen interjects, "and she knew if she provoked the group, somebody was gonna take the bait. She wanted to be punished because her conscious is still eating her up after all these years."

In a separate interview, Dot added:

"Barbara instigated it; she came in the room pushing buttons. Barbara was yelling 'kill me, kill me', because she wanted to die. She wanted somebody to hurt her so she could feel better inside. Her conscience was beating the devil out of her… I was the one who pushed her out of the room and threw her her coat. I made sure she got on the elevator because the media was in the hotel and we didn't want to make a scene."

I cannot say for sure that Barbara was directly involved in Sam's death, but I do believe, as do several other members of my family, she knows what happened that fateful night. To be concerned about her car being seen at the Hacienda motel was strange enough, but to try to provoke a fight some 22 years later, screaming "kill me, kill me" throughout the argument shows that Gwen and Dot's assessment of Barbara may be valid—she harbors guilt over Sam's death and/or her actions since his death. Either way, the royalties she's reaped from Sam's estate seem to be little consolation for the torment she's suffered over the years. As a Christian, I pray for her soul.

*Sam's sisters Mary, Hattie, and Agnes at his induction into the Rock & Roll Hall of Fame,
New York, 1986.*

(Photo courtesy of Agnes Hoskins)

Barbara has managed to live comfortably off of Sam's estate, and to the family's knowledge hasn't worked a day since their marriage in 1959. By the same token, the Cook family has never really understood how they've been excluded from everything. For example, the family found out about the sale of Sam's music catalog in 1985 from a blurb in a music industry magazine, and they were never contacted about any royalties from the sale. The fact that Sam's businesses were absorbed by ABKCO was one thing, but to say there was *nothing* for Sam's parents, brothers and sisters went against everything Sam had discussed with the family years before. When Sam made legal arrangements for his estate, he was a healthy, vibrant young man and had not planned to die for many years to come. As a result, he didn't go into great detail with Papa or his siblings about what he'd established. He told Papa how he had divided his estate and that everyone would be taken care of, but he hadn't given Papa a copy of the will itself. Sometime around 1986, Agnes and the family decided to delve deeper into what happened to Sam's holdings after he died:

"One time Allen Klein was passing through Chicago and invited the whole family to dinner. He knew that we had already contacted an estate attorney, because this attorney had talked to Klein about showing him documents about how he came in control of Sam's holdings, but Klein hadn't given him the papers. The attorney told us to go on and accept the dinner and that this was a perfect opportunity to serve him with a summons."

"The dinner was supposed to be with our attorney, Allen Klein, (his son) Jody, Papa, the brothers and sisters, everybody. We all met downtown (Chicago) at the Drake Hotel. We wanted to subpoena all of ABKCO's records but we didn't tell Klein that. We just told him we felt he had disrespected the Cook family. For example, when my mom died, my dad asked Klein could he pay for the funeral. Instead of sending the money to my dad, he sent it directly to the funeral home. We saw that as a slap in the face. We told him about that and other things we didn't appreciate. We were looking for the attorney to come in to handle the legal stuff and he never showed up. The lawyer was supposed to be presenting Klein with a summons and he never showed up! We tried calling his office from the

Sam's daughter Paula, former love "Dot" Holloway Coates, daughter Sharon, and nieces Gwen, Ophelia, and Doncella, Chicago 2006.

(Photo courtesy of Richard Nichols)

restaurant—figuring maybe he got held up or something—but they said he wasn't there. We haven't seen or heard a word from that attorney since. He wouldn't return our calls; me and Hattie called him constantly for weeks after that. Before that, any time you called his office, they just put you right through, but we never talked to him again after arranging that meeting."

Just like in Sharon Cooke's case, the attorney the Cook family hired started off with the intention of bringing the matter to closure, but for some unexplained reason quit the case, never to be heard from again. The Cook family became frustrated and discouraged and didn't pursue the matter any further.

Sam's children at his gravesite: An emotional Paula Jackson, Joe Cook, and Sharon Cooke,
Glendale, CA, January 2005.

Sam's children pay homage to their father.

(Photos courtesy of Joe Cook)

Sam's grandchildren pose with ex-Soul Stirrer James Phelps: left to right Kenan, twins Kimber and Kira, and Kiyana Bolling.

(Photo courtesy of Agnes Hoskins)

After a certain amount of misdirection in the two previous decades, the early '90's saw focus shift on Sam's gospel material, starting with Specialty's release of "The 2 Sides of Sam Cooke" in 1989. The album featured just what it advertised—Sam's works as both an established Soul Stirrer and early pop artist—and was the first of six Specialty albums featuring Sam's gospel material that would be released in the first half of the decade.

In 1994, ABKCO released "Sam Cooke's SAR Records Story 1959-1965," a 2-CD set that showcased the gospel and pop artists signed to Sam's label. "SAR Records Story" was different from all other compilations because it highlighted Sam's behind-the-scene talents as a writer, producer, and arranger rather than his front-line talents as a vocalist. Sam was as meticulous with the artists on his label as he was with his own music. This attention to detail is highlighted in rare audio snippets as he offers in-studio constructive criticism to his artists as their producer. He sings on only five songs on the two discs—one of those the demo version of "You Send Me"—yet his flavor and direction are apparent on almost every track.

The first CD features gospel works by the Soul Stirrers, (dropped by Specialty Records after Art Rupe lost interest in them), R.H. Harris with his new group, the Paraders, and the Womack Brothers before they made the pop transformation to the Valentinos. Despite the fact that gospel music had lost much of its reverence, and despite the fact Harris and the Soul Stirrers were probably past their prime, their immense talents, in part because of Sam's influence, still shine through in these SAR recordings.

If the first CD is thought of as the more traditional side of SAR, the artists on the second CD represent the movement to mainstream music which was prevalent in the late '50's and early '60's. Artists like the Womack Brothers and Johnnie Taylor were ex-gospel singers. Songs like the Simms Twins' "Soothe Me," the Valentino's "Looking for a Love," and even Sam's "Somewhere There's a Girl," were reworks of gospel songs. SAR was the breeding ground for Sam's creativity and some artists—most notably Mel Carter, Bobby Womack, Johnnie Taylor, and Billy Preston—went on to have distinguished careers. It was Sam's plan to spend more time recruiting new talent and cultivating the current artists on SAR, and with his inspiration, direction, and full attention, the label could have grown to be an R & B powerhouse.

In 1995 Daniel Wolff released the national best-seller, "You Send Me: The Life and Times of Sam Cooke." Wolff's book was more in-depth than Joe McEwen's 1977 biography "Sam Cooke: A Biography in Words & Pictures." Wolff and G. David Tenenbaum exhaustively researched Sam's music career, and in some areas of the book chronicled his life on a day-by-day basis. They interviewed countless Cooke associates and referenced scores of books and articles in an attempt to not only recreate Sam's life, but the political and social climate of the times as well. Despite their efforts, my family couldn't help but focus on one glaring exclusion—our detailed input. Hattie's daughter Ophelia gives her reaction to first seeing the Sam Cooke biography:

"What was disturbing to me was when I saw it on the shelf for the first time. My reaction was 'what is this with my family's history here?' I called my mother and asked her 'did anyone call you? Do you know if anyone talked to Agnes?' because the first thing I noticed was my grandmother's name misspelled (Wolff wasn't sure if her maiden name was "Carl" or "Carroll". It's Carroll), and it made me say 'what's this about? Where did he get his information?'"

I don't fault Wolff, Tenenbaum, or co-writers S. R. Crain and Clifton White for the way they approached their biography. They chose to focus on Sam's colleagues within the music industry, and it probably worked out better that way. It left me with an opportunity to focus on the family point of view and to fill a void in the Sam Cooke saga that may not have been told in its frankness or in its entirety had *they* chosen to pursue it.

Specialty's six gospel album between 1989 and 1994 undoubtedly brought renewed attention to Sam's earlier career. His wondrous gospel achievements had been widely celebrated in the black community for years, yet unheralded in mainstream America. He had always been given credit for his social conscience, his entrepreneurial innovation and his unwavering demand for artistic control, but the quality of his earlier works may have been what influenced the National Academy of Recording Arts and Sciences to grant Sam Cooke a Lifetime Achievement Award at the 1999 Grammy ceremonies.

Fortunately, that same momentum has carried into the 21st century, and it's refreshing to see occasional acknowledgements of Sam Cooke by younger generations. Before Tupac Shakur's death in 1996, for example, he recorded an eerie song called "Thugz Mansion." In the song he consoles his mother from Heaven, telling her not to worry, he's drinking Peppermint Schnapps with Jackie Wilson and Sam Cooke. The introduction to India. Arie's 2001 Grammy-nominated debut album contains a tribute to artists who opened the doors for her, and the first name she mentions is Sam Cooke. She concludes her remembrance of musical "ancestors" by stating "Because of you, a change is gonna come." Spoken word artist Suheir

Hammad pays homage to Sam in "daddy's song," a poem she debuted for her father on Broadway and recites regularly in her performances. Even on the "Survivor" track from his self-titled CD, hardcore rapper Joe Budden admitted that sometimes he needs quiet time alone—"just me and my Sam Cooke tapes."

In 2002, Specialty emptied their vaults to bring the public the 3-CD set "Sam Cooke with the Soul Stirrers, The Complete Specialty Recordings," a chronological collection of Sam's entire gospel and early pop recordings. The 2003 ABKCO re-releases on Super Audio Compact Disc are the most remarkable restorations available to date, and their "Sam Cooke, Portrait of a Legend, 1951-1964" is probably Sam's most definitive single-CD compilation. The documentary DVD "Sam Cooke: Legend" won a 2004 Grammy for Best Longform Music Video, and is the closest the public has come to enjoying a movie based on Sam's life. The abundance of quality material in recent years, along with the convenience of sharing information worldwide via the internet, has helped to preserve Sam's memory and keep his glorious legacy alive.

Sam Cooke was a remarkable human being. His magnetic personality gave him the ability to relate across racial barriers both in music and in life. His foresight and courage allowed him to conquer new heights both as an artist and as a businessman. He possessed unique musical talents, a quest for perfection, and an amazing generosity. He was raised with a fierce tenacity that encouraged him to stand up for what he believed was right, and to fight to the death for what he believed was rightfully his. I'll proudly defend my claim that Sam Cooke was one of the most multi-talented, multi-faceted individuals to have lived in the 20th century. And I am also proud to say that he was *my* Uncle Sam.

Sam's star on the Hollywood Walk of Fame.

(Photo courtesy of Gwendolyn Greene)

Bibliography

Chapter 1
—American Heritage Dictionary, Second College Edition, Boston: Houghton Mifflin, 1985.
—*34 Top 40 hits*... Sam on the Charts: 1957-1966, www.ultimatesamcooke.com.

Chapter 2
—*such musical talents as*...Chicago Landmarks: Wendell Phillips High School, cityofchicago.org.
—*and by the mid-50's*...Chicago: Bronzeville, soulofamerica.com.

Chapter 3
—*65,000 copies*...Wolff, Daniel et al. "You Send Me: The Life & Times of Sam Cooke". New York: Quill/William Morrow, 1995, p. 358.
—*27,000 copies*...Ibid., p. 76-77.
—*increase by 250%*...Katzman, David M., "The Reader's Companion to American History: Black Migration", www.college.hmco.com.
—*18 number one singles*...The Origins of Rock 'n' Roll: 1949-1972, www.menziesera.com.
—*charting 59 R&B singles*...Ibid.
—*topping out at #17*...Ibid.
—*37,000 singles sold*...Wolff et al., "You Send Me", p. 359.

Chapter 4
—*peaking at # 81*...Sam on the Charts: 1957, www.ultimatesamcooke.
   com.
—*would go to #1*...Ibid.
—*would soar to #18*...Ibid.

Chapter 6
—*peaking at #4*...Sam on the Charts: 1958, www.ultimatesamcooke.
   com.

Chapter 7
—*peaking at #22*...Sam on the Charts: 1960, www.ultimatesamcooke.
   com.
—*eventually went to #12*...Ibid.
—*peaking at #17*...Sam on the Charts: 1961, www.ultimatesamcooke.
   com.
—*boosted the song to #4*...Wolff et al.,"You Send Me", SAR Singles:
   1961, p. 376.
—*peaked at #8*... Ibid., SAR Singles: 1962, p. 377.
McEwen, Joe."Sam Cooke: A Biography in Words & Pictures". Sire
   Books/Chappell Music Company, 1977, p. 24.
—*sending the song to #1*...Chubby Checker, www.classicbands.com.
—*all the way to #9*...Sam on the Charts: 1962, www.ultimatesamcooke.
   com.
—*was a smash hit*...Ibid.
—*peaking at #4*...Ibid.
—*went to #12*...Ibid.
—*topped out at #70*...Ibid.
—*heading to #13*...Ibid.
—*His records had sold well here*...Beatles History: October, 1960; Beatles
   History: July, 1961; Beatles History: March, 1962; www.beatles-
   discography.com.

—*#18 R&B, #63 Pop...* Wolff et al., "You Send Me", SAR Singles: 1962, p. 376.

Chapter 8
—*"I think the secret is...* American Bandstand, April 4, 1964.
—*which rose to #31...* Sam on the Charts: 1959, www.ultimatesamcooke. com.
—*peaking at #2...* Ibid., Sam on the Charts: 1960.
—*peaking at #29...* Ibid.
—*The veteran guitarist Clif White...* Wolff et al., "You Send Me", p.146-47.
—*It wasn't until someone...* Ibid., p. 211.
—*went to #9...* Sam on the Charts: 1965, www.ultimatesamcooke.com.
—*1963 is not an end...* Afro-American Almanac: Afro-Voices—"I Have a Dream" by Dr. Martin Luther King, Jr., www.toptags.com.

Chapter 9
—*rising to #44...* Wolff et al., "You Send Me", Derby Singles: 1963, p. 380.
—*peaked at #10...* Sam on the Charts: 1963, www.ultimatesamcooke. com.

Chapter 10
—IMDb: Biography for Allen Klein (mini biography), http://uk.imdb. com.
—*was a turn-off for some...* Beatles History: January 18, 1969, www. beatles-discography.com
—*In 1965,...* The Rolling Stones Worldwide Discography-Agents, Managers, and Record Companies, www.betweentherecords.com.
—*In 1966,...* Beatles History: November 13, 1966, www.beatles-discography.com.
—*But it wasn't until 1969,...* Beatles History: January 28-29, February 3, 1969, www.beatles-discography.com.

—*Their legendary* Abbey Road *album*…Ibid., Beatle Songs: Y.
—*Ray Davies of The Kinks*,…*Ibid.*, Beatles History: January 28, 1969.
—Playboy, November, 1971, p. 104.
—*First of all*,…Official Bobby Darin Website—The Legendary Bobby
    Darin: 45 RPM Records, www.bobbydarin.net/singles.html
—*In "Dream Boogie: The Triumph of Sam Cooke"*,…Guralnick, Peter,
    "Dream Boogie", New York: Little, Brown, and Company, 2005, p.
    466.
— Wolff et al., "You Send Me", p. 283.

Chapter 11
—*peaked at #14* Sam on the Charts: 1963, www.ultimatesamcooke.com.
—*pushing the single to #11*…Ibid.
—*steamrolled to #11*… Ibid., Sam on the Charts: 1964.
—*Within weeks*… Beatles History: May 8, 1969, www.beatles-
    discography.com.
Geller, Larry et al., "If I Can Dream: Elvis' Own Story", New York: Simon
    & Schuster, 1989, p. 183.

Chapter 12
—*There had been*… Barbara Cooke vs. KAGS Music Corp, Case # 912
    365, Superior Court of the State of California for the County of Los
    Angeles, April 6, 1972.
—Guralnick, "Dream Boogie", p. 550.
—*but what he found*…List of Officers, Directors and Agent of Tracey
    Limited, No. 1819-63, State of Nevada, October 14, 1963.
—*The* Articles of Incorporation…Articles of Incorporation of Tracey
    Limited, No. 1819-1963, State of Nevada, October 4, 1963.
—Guralnick, "Dream Boogie", p. 524-25.
—*Also worth noting*,…"Judaism101", www.jewfaq.org/holiday4.htm
—*I've managed to locate*… Articles of Incorporation of Tracey Limited,
    No. 1819-1963, State of Nevada, October 4, 1963.
—*The* List *for the period*… List of Officers, Directors and Agent of

Tracey Limited, No. 1819-63, State of Nevada, April 27, 1964.

—Wolff et al., "You Send Me", p. 316.

—Mysteries & Scandals-The First Season: Sam Cooke (original air date 1/25/99), www.crazyabouttv.com.

—*From the best recreation of events...* Wolff et al., "You Send Me", p. 317-18.

Inquest Held on the Body of Sam Cooke, December 16, 1964. Account of events taken from the official transcript.

Chapter 13

—Seth Pages of Chaos—The Death of Sam Cooke: "Review of the Pathology Report" by Rodney Muhammad, www.khemet.net.

Young, Paul. "L.A. Exposed: Who Killed Sam Cooke?" New York: Thomas Dunne Books/St. Martin's Press, 2002, p. 102-03.

—*When Fuller's uncle...* Ibid., p. 273.

—*But on July 18,...* Ibid., p. 111-113

—*no evidence of foul play...* Aaron Poehler's Music Journalism Archives: The Strange Case of Bobby Fuller (part 2), www.angelfire.com/in2/aaronmusicarchives.

—*Someone asked him...* Young, "L.A. Exposed", p. 112.

—Guralnick, "Dream Boogie", p. 622.

—"*It was snowing hard in New York*"...Ibid. p. 622.

—*What is clear...* The New York Times: "Traffic Snarled by Rain and Fog: Flights Canceled, Turnpike Shut and Ship Grounded", December 13, 1964, p. 85.

—*According to the U.S. Weather Bureau's forecast...* Ibid., "U.S. Weather Bureau Report", p. 1, December 11, 1964.

—*and the actual temperature...* Ibid., "U.S. Weather Bureau Report", p.1, December 12, 1964.

—*Even going back...* Ibid., "Weather Reports Throughout the United States", p.94, December 10, 1964.

—Guralnick, "Dream Boogie", p. 622.

—Wolff et al., "You Send Me", p. 323.

—Guralnick, "Dream Boogie", p. 623-24.

—*However…*The Los Angeles Sentinel: "Double Funeral Set For Cooke", December 17, 1964, p. A1, A2.

—Wolff et al., "You Send Me", p. 323.

—*Klein saw an open door…*Certificate of Amendment of Articles of Incorporation of Tracey Limited, No. 1819-63, State of Nevada, January 4, 1965.

—*The* List of Officers…List of Officers, Directors and Agent of Tracey Records Limited (formerly) Tracey Limited, No. 1819-63, State of Nevada, June 17, 1965.

—*The next year…*List of Officers, Directors and Agent of Tracey Records Limited, No. 1819-63, State of Nevada, signed July, 20, 1966.

—*In March of 1970…*Certificate of Merger of ABKCO-Klein Corp., et al. into ABKCO-Klein Corp., Document No. 824303, New York Department of State, March 31, 1970.

—Jet Magazine: "Record Sale Spurt Adds $150,000 to Cooke Estate", Jan. 21, 1965, p.61.

—Geller et al., "If I Can Dream", p. 184.

—*Autopsy Physician Dr. Harold Kade testified…*Inquest Held on the Body of Sam Cooke, December 16, 1964.

—*Despite the results…*Ibid.

Chapter 14

—Wolff et al., "You Send Me", p. 350-51.

—*Two of Klein's early associates…*Dopson, Roger and Johnny Vallis. "Buddy Knox: A Texas Gentleman", www.rockabillyhall.com/ BuddyKnox1.html.

—*Levy, who had reputed ties…*WMOB: The Wiretap Network. "The Frank & Fritzy Show-Morris Levy", www.wmob.com/cast.html.

Feldman, Lawrence E. "Mp3 and Vietnam", www.virtualrecordings.com/ vietnam.htm.

Acknowledgements

I CAN'T EXPRESS TO YOU the range of emotions I experienced writing most of this book– from the pride I felt of Sam standing up for equality as an entertainer and rising to the top of his craft, to the love I heard in the voices of my relatives as they described treasured moments spent with Sam, to the despair I shared with Sam as he realized that he had cracked the glass ceiling only to find a concrete one above, to the anger I harbored at those who not only killed my uncle, but were hateful enough to scandalize his name. It hurt me to write this book because if for no other reason, I should be by his side helping him write his memoirs instead of recording the memories of an uncle I never knew.

As emotional as this experience was, I thank those of you who help keep Sam's memory alive, and for making my family and I realize that more than just our lives were affected by his presence and his music. In a way, it revived memories that had lain dormant in us for a long time. It had been years since I thought about my mom's "Saturday Morning Revue" and it wasn't until I began to write did I consciously realize how Sam's music has been there for me throughout different stages of my life.

My cousin Eugene Jamison was a key component of this book because as a young man he was either there firsthand or soaked up the many stories my aunts and uncles told about Sam over the years. Either way, Gene was able to recall certain events about Sam's life even when they couldn't or weren't around to do so. In addition, he was privy to the results of many years of investigative work his father conducted on Sam until he himself passed away. Gene had this to say about renewed interest in Sam over the past few years:

"It's good to see Sam move again. All the days we spent in the wings of the Regal, a lot of his movements, like Sam walking out to the curtain and snapping his fingers, and June Gardner would be right there on it like you wouldn't believe, I had forgotten about those things. Sam would make certain little gestures (Gene put his hand up, then down, then out, making a drum sound with every movement) and June was right there. He had these subtle little movements I had forgotten all about."

Special thanks go to the family members closest to Sam—most notably Charles, Agnes and David—for their candor and honesty. I know that while they shared many warm and happy memories of Sam, time has still not healed their loss completely. On several occasions they shared stories that had been repressed for years, and quite often these memories were the most painful. I sometimes had to readdress certain topics in order to get the whole story, and it's important to let my relatives know I appreciate their resolve in enduring the unpleasant. I grew to understand that tasks I initially took for granted–talking about Sam's death, looking through old boxes and photo albums for pictures, and talking about life without Sam–required an extreme emotional expenditure on their part.

I'd like to thank my mother, Gwendolyn Greene, and my wife, Augustine Greene. Their computer expertise helped make editing the pictures, cover, and manuscript text a less taxing affair—on my part that is. I know the perfectionist in me pestered them to no ends, and I am grateful for their patience. I'd also like to thank my cousin Toni Howard not only for her creative feedback, but for her willingness to share many of the photos from her late mother Barbara's collection.

Rest in peace my cousin Charlene "Cookie" Graham, whose life was tragically taken from us by a drunk driver on, of all days, December 11, 2004. Your infectious smile and upbeat personality will forever warm our hearts.

Special thanks go to Zelda Sands, who helped provide a West Coast perspective while most of Sam's family was here in Chicago. Sam's story never would have come together completely without her. Sam always held Zelda in high regards, and now I see why.

Special thanks go to G. David Tenenbaum, who did a great deal of the research behind Daniel Wolff's earlier biography, "You Send Me." David is a true Cookie that devoted over twelve years of his life, almost to the point of obsession at times, to complete his manuscript. If ever there was an example of a "labor of love," it describes the time and effort he put forth to bring his book to fruition. He never hesitated in helping me along the way, constantly providing me with facts, documentation, and contacts.

Christopher Pfeiffer is owed a world of thanks for helping a novice writer understand the nuances of the writing and publishing processes. It's one thing to sit at a computer and bang out a manuscript; it's another thing to know what to do with it afterward.

Last but not least, I'd once again like to thank the Sam Cooke Fan Club. As much as I love Sam's music, I'm not nearly an expert on it, and sometimes I leaned on its members around the world to help me through certain parts of this book. Donald Piper, Rodney Muhammad, Eli Williams, Jr. and Kevin Trumper were especially helpful, and their love and mastery of Sam's music is no less than overwhelming. Thank you all.

–Erik Greene

Printed in the United States
By Bookmasters